Cover design
by GABRIELLE BEAULIEU, s.g.m.

DATE 3 NOVEMBRE 1993
ISBN 2-920965-02-6
Dépôt légal-Bibliothèque nationale du Québec, 1993
Dépôt légal-Bibliothèque nationale du Canada, 1993

Estelle Mitchell, s.g.m.
Member of The Montreal Historical Society
The Canadian Authors' Society
and The International Council on Archives

THE SPIRITUEL PORTRAIT

OF

SAINT MARGUERITE D'YOUVILLE
1701-1771

Translated from the French Original by Sister Joanna Kerwin, Grey Nun of the Sacred Heart, Philadelphia and Sister Antoinette Bezaire, Grey Nun of Montreal.

BY THE SAME AUTHOR:

- **Marguerite d'Youville**
  Palm Publisher, Montreal 1965
      Translated from:
      Elle a beaucoup aimé
      Fides, Montréal et Paris

- **Mère Jane Slocombe**
      Fides 1964, Montréal et Paris

- **Messire Pierre Boucher**
  Montréal, Librairie Beauchemin, 1967
  Vac Offset Inc. 1980

- **Le soleil brille à minuit**
  Montréal, Librairie Beauchemin, 1970

- **From the Fatherhood of God to the Brotherhood of Mankind**
  Vac Offset & Printing, Montreal 1977
      Translated by Joanna Kerwin from
      French edition,
      Le Vrai Visage de Marguerite d'Youville
      Montréal, Librairie Beauchemin,
      1973, 1974, 1978
      Japanese translation, October 1978
      Portuguese translation, 1980
      Spanish translation: Altagracia A. Contreras, 1990

- **Love Spans the Centuries, Vol. IV, 1877-1910**
  Meridian Press 1987
      Translated by Antoinette Bezaire, s.g.m.
      from French edition,
      Essor apostolique
      Montréal, Tupo Graphica, 1981

- **Le curé Charles Youville-Dufrost et sa mère, 1729-1790**
  Éditions du Méridien, Montréal 1991
  English translation by Sr. A. Bézaire, 1993

This book published in 1977 under the title: **From the Fatherhood of God to the Brotherhood of Mankind** was printed in 1993 under a new title: **The Spiritual Portrait of Saint Marguerite d'Youville.**

Mother Marguerite,

*It was our desire and our dream...
to walk along the way you followed,
to seek you in the words of those who
knew you, studying your letters,
sensing your very soul.*

*In a word to see more clearly the
cherished face of the woman you were
of the woman you became when it
pleased God to show you clearly that
he is our Father and all men are
brothers.*

PREFACE (1)

"Few figures in our religious history have had as many biographers as Blessed Marguerite d'Youville." This statement, true as it is, shows the popular appeal of this great and noble woman in our country's history.

It is enough to have even a superficial knowledge of the history of Montreal to realize the influence Mme d'Youville exerted on the people of her time and how important a rôle she played both under French rule and under British domination, for she lived during both these periods with all their difficulties and uncertainties.

Nor did her influence end with her death. It showed itself in various ways and has continued especially through the growth and influence of the community she founded. Like Mother d'Youville, the "Grey Nuns" are part of our history and some of them have written unforgettable pages in the history of our religion. We need only think of those "heroic women" of the Far North.

There is no lack, then, of "Lives" of Mme d'Youville, beginning with the biography written by her son, abbé Charles Dufrost. After him, several writers were attracted by her personality and by her life, filled as it was with good works of every kind.

The book I have the honor and the pleasure to introduce is not meant to replace these numerous and generally well-written biographies; it presupposes them, for it belongs on another level. Sister Estelle Mitchell did not intend to write of Marguerite d'Youville's life and works but rather of her spiritual development, of God's irresistible presence in her life as wife and religious. The author's purpose was to describe her pilgrimage to the mountain of holiness, a pilgrimage now officially recognized by the Church in the beatification and — soon, we hope — in the canonization of this rare and holy woman.

Blessed Marguerite d'Youville as presented in this Preface has since been inscribed in the catalogue of saints by His Holiness John Paul II on December 9, 1990.

The intent to paint the spiritual portrait of a person like Marguerite d'Youville may seem to be a daring and interesting, even fascinating undertaking. Every attempt of this kind is worthwhile and valuable for it shows that the men and women who labored with might and main to build our Church and our country were made of flesh and blood like us. Their heroism and holiness was lived out day by day in ordinary circumstances. Theirs was a long and at times painful road.

In Mother d'Youville we find ourselves incontestably faced with a woman of action, the living example of the "valiant woman" described in Scripture, as those who knew her remind us. M. Faillon wrote: "Mme d'Youville's work of caring for the unfortunate, her inexhaustible charity, her courageous and generous zeal, and all her other unusual qualities can give us the right to entitle her biography "Canada's Valiant Woman.""

Her works prove that she was a woman of action — one who had a gift for organization. She was a hospital administrator who, by reason of her position, dealt with both civil and religious authorities and was obliged at times to justify or defend herself before them. But also and especially, she was a person of unconquerable faith and hope, a woman of prayer and a true religious. There can be no authentic holiness without union with God, without a mystical relationship. Her devoted service, her charitable activities are only the reflection, the clear sign of the love of God which motivated her to the point of complete forgetfulness of self.

Because of her many works, Mme d'Youville could be called "Mother of Universal Charity." Her zeal, indeed, knew no limits, from abandoned babies to sick old men. Every human suffering, both physical and spiritual, struck a chord of sympathy in her, evoking compassion and sensitive, motherly attention. In the Decree of Beatification, his

Holiness, Pope John XXIII recalled: "Her house was open to everyone who suffered from poverty, illness or other affliction, without distinction of age, nationality, sex or religion, for Marguerite wanted her love to have no limits. When war ravaged the country, doubling her efforts, she took in wounded soldiers, providing them with every possible kind of relief; she opened her door to fugitives, dogged by hunger and poverty, feeding them in ways that sometimes bordered on the miraculous; to foundlings whose number had grown considerably, she showed herself a loving, kind mother. Pouring out on all her treasures of supernatural love, she deserved the title Mother of Universal Charity."

Her charity was universal and heroic because of its tirelessness and because of certain deeds which surpass human ability and are possible only with strength from on high. Such love, moreover, could not exist without supernatural faith and hope of like intensity. The life of the theological virtues around which Christian holiness develops is all one: growth in charity presupposes and requires growth in theological faith and hope.

If we study Mother d'Youville's spiritual life attentively, we must notice an increasing growth in the supernatural virtues of faith and hope. Her work, it has been said, was a ministry of charity to all men; we might add that it was also a mystical way of hope which became trust and heroic abandonment to Divine Providence.

Slowly and progressively the Lord prepared Marguerite Dufrost, later Mme d'Youville, to become this "Mother of Universal Charity." Through the events of her life, God purified the young woman, the wife, the religious. He perfected her especially by suffering, — bodily suffering — and suffering of the spirit and the heart. Mme d'Youville came to know the "night of the senses" and the "night of the spirit" of which St. John of the Cross, in particular, *wrote. Her experience was unlike that of Teresa of Avila. It was her own, in accordance with God's purpose and in harmony with the work Providence intended for her.*

From the time of her conversion, she moved continually forward. But this was rather the "second conversion" when, in Tauler's words, the soul "is turned again towards God." With the help of her spiritual directors, certainly, and especially as her life unfolded before her, she discovered her "way," her own spirituality centered on abandonment to the Providence of the Eternal Father.

This devotion to the Eternal Father, Providence of the poor, was at the heart of her mission, as was her devotion to the Cross of Jesus. Born, in a sense, from her own suffering, it developed as she grew familiar with the daily sufferings of others.

Fortitude was probably Mother d'Youville's dominant moral virtue, rooted in her devotion to the Eternal Father, flowering at the foot of the suffering Savior's cross.

Faillon wrote: "She was especially called to spread devotion to the Eternal Father as the Source of all love and compassion for human suffering through the Religious Institute she founded." The Litany to the Eternal Father, she had composed, remains as witness to the central point of her spiritual life and a legacy to those who would continue her work.

Need we add that love for the poor, which is so central to Mother d'Youville's ministry, can exist only with love of poverty for Jesus' sake? Hope and poverty are two virtues, two attitudes which depend on each other. Theological hope finds its purity, its transparency (which is its perfection) in spiritual poverty. St. John of the Cross teaches us in the Ascent of Mount Carmel (Book III, ch. 14):

"We hope only for what we do not yet possess; the less the soul possesses other things, the more it is able and apt

*to hope for what it desires, and, consequently, the greater
its hope. On the other hand, the more it possesses other
things, the less apt and able it is to hope, and thus, the
weaker its hope."*

Was not Mother d'Youville's love for the poor, then,
requiring at times heroic virtue, in the final analysis the
expression of trust in God which filled her being? Hope
became trusting and total abandonment. The Te Deum she
recited before the smoking ruins of the hospital points out
to us how far her pilgrimage had led her. Abandonment,
at this point in her life, went beyond simple resignation
and submission to God's action. It involved now active
cooperation, a real asceticism which we might call mystical.
For now, even while respecting God's freedom of action,
the soul gives itself unreservedly to His penetrating love.
The Holy Spirit acts visibly with His gifts in the soul.

In summary, we might say of Mother d'Youville what
St. Paul wrote of Abraham: "Though it seemed Abraham's
hope could not be fulfilled, he hoped and he believed,
and through doing so he did become the father of many
nations exactly as he had been promised" (Rom. 4:18).

Our times, characterized by the cult of efficiency and
sometimes of activism, need now more than ever the witness
of this woman who knew how to combine action and contemplation. She reminds us, by her very life, of the great law
of the apostolate set down by St. Paul: "If I give away
all that I possess, piece by piece, and if I even let them take
my body to burn it, but am without love, it will do me
no good whatever" (I Cor. 13:3).

Sister Mitchell deserves our thanks and praise for
having helped us to understand still more deeply the
wealth of this remarkable woman's spiritual life and
holiness. Thus one of her daughters helps us to discover
the spiritual portrait of this "Mother" — the authentic
face of Marguerite.

Roland Dorris, P.S.S.

FOREWORD

Marguerite d'Youville did not have time to record her spiritual life in either a diary or a lengthy correspondence. This is regrettable. Eighty-nine letters, five memoranda, the document known as the Original Commitment and two wills constitute the only sources she signed and left to posterity. Furthermore, these letters scarcely encouraged the expression of personal reflections, for they were hastily written and deal largely with administrative matters. All but three of them were written during the last ten years of her life, and many passages do convey the atmosphere in which her interior life developed. This is particularly true when we pause to reflect on the events which caused her to write them.

But this scarcity of documents is compensated by the abundance of her works. For Marguerite d'Youville spoke especially through them. What wonderful things we might have learned if she had told us herself about the development of God's life in her. She did not have time for this precisely because her charism urged her to act. This was not the feverish and confused action we call activism, but rather action inspired by love and aimed at expressing love. And this activity was inspired by her contemplation; for by looking at God, the Father of all, Marguerite understood the bonds of brotherhood uniting her to the members of the whole human family. She realized that the love shown by Providence "which provides for everything" (letter of Sept. 21, 1771) is essentially love that gives freely.

And she modeled herself on this love. Thus, how important it is for anyone who wants to examine her life to take into account not merely her reluctant personal disclosures but more especially the spirit of initiative and the organizational ability which characterized her work. Her work was to help the needy around her — her brothers and sisters.

The scarcity of written documentation is compensated also by the testimony of Marguerite's contemporaries who witnessed her spiritual growth and were her close friends. Their testimony is all the more precious in that it describes the influences which formed her. It lets us put into perspective the outstanding traits of her personality and enter into the events which marked her life. Serious historians have made use of their testimony in the works incorporated in the Summarium of the Beatification proceedings. This book is based on them. They are, in chronological order:

Vie de Mme d'Youville, fondatrice des Soeurs de la Charité, à Montréal, by abbé Charles Dufrost, the Foundress' son. This manuscript is preserved in the general archives of the Grey Nuns.

Mémoire pour servir à la vie de Mme d'Youville, principally derived from the statements of Sisters Despins, La Source, Rainville, Mme Gamelin and of another Sister. Compiled by Charles Dufrost and preserved in the general archives of the Grey Nuns.

Charles Dufrost was born July 18, 1729 and died March 7, 1790. He drew up his first *Mémoire* around 1777 (Summarium of the Cause of Beatification, p. 110). Three years later, he collated the statements of Marguerite d'Youville's first companions and of her sister, Mme Ignace Gamelin. Since his first manuscript includes details of Mme d'Youville's childhood, we can conclude that he acquired his information from the members of his mother's family, from her sister, Mme Clémence Maugras, from her brother, abbé Joseph Dufrost and also from Marguerite d'Youville herself.

Recueil des Règles et Constitutions à l'usage des filles séculières administratices de l'hôpital général de Montréal, dites les Soeurs de la charité, recueillies sur les anciens titres et usages de la Communauté, by M. Etienne Montgolfier, p.s.s., Dec. 2, 1776.

After his arrival in Montreal in 1751, M. Montgolfier was superior of the Seminary, vicar general of the Diocese of Quebec, ecclesiastical superior of the Grey Nuns, and was thus in a position to speak with some authority of the spirit of the Congregation and of its Foundress' personality.

Vie de Mme d'Youville, fondatrice et première supérieure des Soeurs de la Charité ou 'Soeurs Grises' by M. Antoine Sattin, p.s.s., July 20, 1829.

M. Sattin arrived in Montreal Sept. 1, 1794. He had the good fortune to know eight of Marguerite d'Youville's first Sisters well, and also Sr. Marie-Louise O'Flaherty, the orphan welcomed by the Foundress in 1757 who became a Grey Nun in 1776. M. Sattin compiled the testimony of her contemporaries and it is thanks to him that the words of the Foundress were preserved.

Vie de Mme d'Youville, fondatrice des Soeurs de la Charité de Villemarie dans l'Ile de Montréal, en Canada. Tours, 1852. M. Faillon was able to interview the last generation of Sisters who had known Marguerite d'Youville's contemporaries. Further, he was in a position to consult "the papers which we have here, in France, in the archives of the government and elsewhere", (letter of Sept. 22, 1851 to Mother

Rose Coutlée). M. Faillon was the first to analyze the ways God worked out His purposes in Marguerite d'Youville and also her ways of dealing with the community. On this work, highly recommended by Rome, the author has based much of what follows.

Vie de la Vénérable Marie-Marguerite Du Frost de Lajemmerais, veuve d'Youville, 1701 — 1771, by Albertine Ferland-Angers, of the Historical Society of Montreal; Librairie Beauchemin Limited, Montreal, 1945.

One hundred fifty-nine of the three hundred eighty-six pages of this biography are devoted to an appendix containing Marguerite d'Youville's letters and documents of prime importance concerning the Foundress and her congregation.

Apostolic Letters of His Holiness John XXIII, declaring the venerable servant of God, Marie-Marguerite Dufrost de Lajemmerais Blessed, May 3, 1959.

PRINCIPAL STEPS IN MARGUERITE D'YOUVILLE'S CAUSE OF CANONIZATION

1884; 1885:   Informative process in Montreal.

1890:   Introduction of the Cause in Roman Court.

1894:   Decree of non-cult.

1901:   Decree of renown for holiness.

1910:   The process of virtues and miracles recognized as valid.

1927:   Ante-preparatory Congregation.

1931:   Preparatory Congregation at the end of which an historical study is requested.

1950:   The historical work is approved by the Sacred Congregation of Rites.

1953:   Second Preparatory Congregation.

1955:   Decree of the Heroicity of Virtues.

1959:   Decree "De tuto".

1959, May 3: Beatification.

1990, Dec. 9: Canonization

PRINCIPAL DATES IN THE LIFE OF
BLESSED MARGUERITE D'YOUVILLE

October 15, 1701:
   Birth at Varennes, Quebec, Canada
   Baptism the following day in the parish church of St. Anne of Varennes.

August, 1712:
   Student at the Ursuline Convent in Quebec until 1714.

August 12, 1722:
   Marriage to François You de la Découverte in Notre Dame Church, Montreal

1727:
   Exceptional grace: devotion to the Eternal Father becomes the focal point of her life.
   She joins the Confraternity of the Holy Family.

July 4, 1730:
   François d'Youville dies at thirty years of age, leaving her with two sons, François and Charles, both of whom were to become priests.

October 23, 1731:
   Mme d'Youville enrolls in the Confraternity of the Sacred Heart, established in the chapel of the Ursulines of Quebec. October 23 is the day set aside for her to "fulfill her obligations to the heart of Christ."

Mach 16, 1733:
   She becomes a member of the Confraternity of the Blessed Sacrament and of a holy death.

September 28, 1737:

Rental of the dwelling known as the "LeVerrier house" to be "occupied the following October 1."[1] On October 31,[2] along with her companions, Louise Thaumur de la Source, Catherine Cusson and Catherine Demers, she commits herself to the service of the poor before a small statue known as Our Lady of Providence.

November 21, 1737:

The women welcome their first boarder, Françoise Auzon, a sixty-year-old blind woman.

December 31, 1737:

Mme d'Youville and her companions privately make religious profession.

1741:

Mme d'Youville commissions a painting of the Eternal Father in France. She attributes to him the cure of Father Normant P.S.S., protector of the early beginnings of their work.

January 31, 1745:

Fire in the LeVerrier house. Mme d'Youville promises her poor she will not abandon them.

1. Historians, have placed the event in 1738 because of the statement of Charles Dufrost. However, the following evidence weakens this assertion: the discovery of the lease of the LeVerrier house, dated September 28, 1737; the admission of Françoise Auzon, Mme d'Youville's first boarder the following November 21 (handwritten document no. 146 in the archives of the Grey Nuns of Montreal); and finally the proof that the Sisters lived together under the same roof (Adhémar Registry, document no. 351). Moreover, Charles was only eight years old at the time.

2. It is usually thought that the religious profession took place October 30. However, Charles Dufrost states in the two documents he wrote about his mother "the eve of All Saints' Day" and hence October 31, not October 30.

February 2, 1745:
> With her first companions, she signs the act of total renunciation and complete self-dedication, known as Original Commitment.

October 7, 1747:
> As administrator she takes over the General Hospital of the Charon Brothers.

October 15, 1750:
> Mme d'Youville is dismissed from her post as administrator.

June 3, 1753:
> Letters patent granted by Louis XV, re-instating her as administrator.

June 15, 1755:
> Approbation of the community by Bishop de Pontbriand.

August 25, 1755:
> Clothing ceremony of the first Grey Nuns.

1756:
> Bigot, the Intendant, commits to Mme d'Youville the care of wounded French soldiers and of English prisoners of war.

October 8, 1757:
> Seriously ill, Mme d'Youville makes her will.

June 18, 1759:
> Death of M. Normant du Faradon P.S.S.

July 24, 1759:
> Charles, Mme d'Youville's son and parish priest of Pointe-Lévy, is taken prisoner by the English.

September 8, 1760:
> Montreal surrenders to the English army.

May 18, 1765:
: The General Hospital is destroyed by fire. Mme d'Youville invites her companions to say the Te Deum with her "to thank God for the cross he has just sent us". Then and there, she decides to rebuild the institution.

April 4, 1770:
: Mme d'Youville initiates the daily recitation of the Invocations to the Eternal Father, composed by M. Pierre Huet de Lavalinière P.S.S., at her request.

1771:
: At the beginning of the year, Mme d'Youville falls seriously ill (letter of M. Montgolfier to Bishop Briand, March 8, 1771). She seems fully recovered a few months later (letter of May 6, 1771).

December 9, 1771:
: First attack of paralysis.

December 13, 1771:
: Second attack of paralysis.

December 14, 1771:
: She makes her will and leaves her Sisters her spiritual testament.

December 23, 1771:
: Monday evening at about half past eight she dies in the arms of Sister Despins.

December 26, 1771:
: Burial in the crypt of the General Hospital.

Correspondence

Eighty-nine letters written by Marguerite d'Youville of which three were written in 1751 and the others from 1762 to 1771.

Letter of M. Henri-François Gravé, director of the Seminary of Quebec, dated Jan. 5, 1772 and addressed to Mother Thérèse Lemoyne-Despins, second Superior General of the Grey Nuns. M. Gravé lived in Montreal from 1759 to 1761 during which time he was chaplain of the General Hospital.

Letters of Mother Thérèse Lemoyne-Despins, dated Aug. 13, Sept. 9, Sept. 10, Sept. 16, and Sept. 17, 1772 and addressed to various correspondents, to whom she gave a detailed account of the death of Marguerite d'Youville and expressed her admiration for the Foundress whom she had known since 1739.

Letters of M. E. Montgolfier P.S.S., to Bishop O. Briand, of Quebec, Mar. 8 and May 6, 1771.

N.B. The complete bibliography at the end of this volume indicates the other sources used.

The reader who is unfamiliar with Marguerite d'Youville's life will find it helpful to consult first one of the biographies of the Foundress.

Chapter I

TOWARD THE FATHER

> "If I were to die tonight and were
> asked what the most moving thing
> in this world is for me, I would
> probably say that it is God's activity
> in the souls of men."
>
> Julien Green

To those around her, God's activity in Marguerite's soul was obvious. They noted the exact year in which it occurred and the effects it had on the twenty-six-year-old woman. "Three years before her husband's death, she obviously turned away from the vanities of the world and chose the path of piety," [1] Charles Dufrost noted in his two manuscripts. "Suddenly, an extraordinary change took place in her," remarked her second biographer, M. Sattin, adding immediately that this "fortunate change" occurred three years before the death of François d'Youville. [2] Faillon, the historian, corroborated this statement and situated the event "five years after Madame d'Youville's marriage," [3] August 12, 1722.

---

1. Typewritten copies of Charles Dufrost's manuscripts, pp. 2 & 4. Marguerite d'Youville's son was born in 1729; thus, he did not witness this occurrence but heard of it either from his mother herself or from her contemporaries.
2. Sattin, p. 11. François d'Youville died July 4, 1730.
3. Faillon, p. 16.

Finally, Marguerite herself removed all uncertainty; she dated this unusual grace at the beginning of 1727. "For almost forty years," she wrote on October 12, 1766, "the Divine Father has been the object of all my trust." [4] This 'almost' is in itself significant, indicating how important to Marguerite d'Youville was the day when trust in the Eternal Father took root in her. This experience radically changed her vision of the world. Any attempt to explain her reactions, her pioneering work, and the constant ideal it expressed must look for an explanation to this transformation reaching to the depths of her being.

When she recalled this experience at the end of her life, God's purpose for her had been fulfilled. She was waiting for the final summons of the Lord. Forty years earlier she had responded to His invitation and now her soul was at peace, open to love and filled with love.

If only she had added an account of the details of the circumstances surrounding this sudden experience of God. Was it when she was at prayer or while she was engaged in her daily work? Questions for which we do not have answers; for Marguerite "reflected a great deal but spoke little", [5] as her son assures us. When she spoke, however, her words were filled with meaning, fruitful with years of silence. Her disclosures have been compiled and carefully recorded and placed in their historical context, they focus a clear light on her personality. But the deepest mystery of her soul escapes the most extensive investigation. For Marguerite d'Youville,

---

4. Letter to the abbé de l'Isle-Dieu, Vicar General of the diocese of Québec, living in France.
5. Dufrost, 1st manuscript, p. 2.

as for so many other people, the most beautiful moments of her life would be those she relived only in the depths of a soul filled with gratitude. Yet even while we respect her reticence, we can reconstruct what her life was like before she opened her soul to joy. No one experiences this joy unless he has first accepted the cross of suffering. Only the Holy Spirit reveals the mysterious joy which lies in wait for those who accept the cross. This joy then transforms them.

In 1727, Madame d'Youville "shed very bitter tears, the more bitter because she understood the meaning of resignation so poorly". [6] She was the victim of an apparently desperate situation. Here we have one of her rare personal disclosures. Who else could have mentioned "bitter tears"! And who else could have explained their cause so accurately? No need to be surprised at her suffering. The young woman could not even hide her misfortune, so obvious were the failings of François d'Youville, the fur trader. Her closest friends must have found it easy to pity her, even if they did not perhaps completely understand that this trial forced her to challenge the very meaning of her life and to beg for an explanation of her suffering. It would have been hopelessly naive to keep hoping for a real change of heart in François. For in her husband's heart there was no longer room for anyone but himself. Fickle, selfish, indifferent, he had thrown off all responsibility while Marguerite was forced to work hard to support herself as she lacked at times even the bare necessities of life. [7] It must have been sad to live in this home, for François returned there only when other doors were closed to him. And

---

6. Dufrost, ibid., p. 5.
7. Sattin, p. 10.

sadder still when Marguerite stayed at the farmhouse at Bout-de-l'Ile — as she did at least early in
1727. [8] What other explanation can we give for the
fact that Louise, a baby only a few months old, was
buried at Pointe-Claire on March 1 of that same
year? [9]

Of her five children, three had died in infancy.
This last death must have played a part in the crisis
of faith; "there are few mothers who loved their
children as tenderly as Madame d'Youville," her son,
Charles, would say. [10] Marguerite's last hopes
crumbled under the weight of this trial. Until then
she had kept on believing that better days would
come. For instance, on the death of Madame You de
la Découverte, [11] François might have reformed
and given up his illegal trade on claiming his
inheritance. A vain hope. He wasted the money in
gambling. [12] Loneliness, frustration, solitude were
Marguerite's companions. And this isolation was all
the more painful "because she never stopped loving
her husband although he caused her great suffering." [13]

8. This farmhouse at Bout-de-l'Ile was used as a shelter by
   Pierre You's sons between their dangerous trips to Ile-
   aux-Tourtes; there Philippe and François carried on their
   fur trade with the Indians.

9. Since the Youville house was not far from the cemetery, the
   infant would have been buried there if the family had been
   living in Montreal.

10. Dufrost, op. cit., p. 7. François and Marguerite had six
    children in all, but in 1727 only four had been born.

11. Sattin mentions that Mme de la Decouverte's death occurred
    shortly after Marguerite's marriage. The records of Notre
    Dame Parish give no date of burial.

12. François is said to have been a compulsive gambler and card-
    player. (Angers, p. 38)

13. Sattin, p. 11.

She expressed her love discreetly, for François' pride would not have tolerated explanations much less reproaches. She kept absolute silence about his strange conduct exercising forethought, tenderness and solicitude "to provide for everything" to lighten the burden she and her children were to him. Nothing succeeded in bringing him back to her. There was overwhelming proof that the love he had vowed for her was dead. Still, somewhere in her husband's heart there might be a path she had not yet been able to find. What was the basic cause of the tragedy of loneliness — after they had promised to love one another for better and for worse? Poverty, a life filled with work held no surprises for Marguerite; for a long time she had been accustomed to this.

But there was one thing which meant more to her than anything else for which she could not be consoled — love, the union of hearts and minds. Forty years later she spoke of it in unmistakeable terms. "Nothing can equal the happiness of a united home. All the good things on earth cannot approach this happiness," she would write. [14] Weighed down by unhappiness, facing the prospect that it would continue for years to come, she felt her courage waver. She experienced her own weakness, a precious experience which would make her sensitive to others' weakness. Most of all, she realized that she had reached a fork in the road where a choice must be made. She could drop all her weapons, wear herself out in useless regret, wall herself up in indifference toward François and be satisfied with the meager joys that life might still hold for her. Or she could agree to forget all her ambitions

---

14. Letter to M. et Mme de Figuery, Aug. 20, 1766.

and her projects in an act of complete trust. She could give God not only the past but even more, the present and the future. In her anguish Marguerite cried out to God. And the God Who is close to broken hearts and battered spirits (Ps. 34:19) answered her. As though a brilliant light lit up her darkness, she knew that this best of all Fathers loved her. He held her destiny in His hands, His providence was all around and He would support her as she walked along this unknown way to which He called her.

Apparently this invitation from God presented itself to her as a summons. Marguerite's destiny was decided the moment she chose what is eternal, turning aside from transitory things. The whole experience happened without any external phenomena witnessing to God's action in her. Perhaps this explains Marguerite's silence about it. Then again, she was one of those strong personalities who are able to keep their joys and sorrows to themselves. Characteristically, she would express the secret of her soul by deeds rather than by words. For now she had reached, so to speak, a new and higher level of life, one based on the realities of faith.

Scarcely had she experienced this illumination than "the world, the pleasures of society" lost their attractiveness in her eyes. Marguerite freely gave up the "vain adornments" she had worn to such advantage. It was said that she was "one of the most beautiful women of her time." But now she realized that the desire for the things of God leaves no room for compromises. Her contemporaries became aware of this change in her and were amazed. Until then, Madame d'Youville, an exemplary Catholic, had not neglected her religious duties. But from the moment God revealed Himself to her, her every desire was centered on Him.

Marguerite's course of action revealed that her spiritual adventure was guided by a spirit of detachment and humility. Aware of the dangers of pride and illusion, she asked the advice of M. du Lescoät, a Sulpician, the pastor of Notre Dame Parish. [15] As her "guide in this new way of life", this man of experience and outstanding holiness [16] recognized the authenticity of the grace she had received and fostered God's work in her by guiding her in the way of trust and of abandonment in the hands of the Heavenly Father. He discerned to some degree the extraordinary vocation for which she was destined and spoke prophetically to her: "God destines you to raise up a house which will be in its decline."[17]

Twenty years would elapse before the prediction was verified. When she assumed the administration of the General Hospital, Madame d'Youville mentioned his prophecy. Contemplating God's eternal Fatherhood aroused in her an unwavering

---

15. The quotations are excerpts from Sattin's *Life*.

16. M. du Lescoät was born at St-Malo in 1689 and arrived in Montreal in 1717. He was pastor of Notre Dame from 1725 to 1730 and died at the age of fourty-four. "He was a great man and a saint", M. Montgolfier wrote of him. Popular devotion made his grave a place of pilgrimage and several miraculous cures were attributed to him. (Ferland-Angers, Dictionnaire biographique canadien 2, p. 431).

17. Dufrost (p. 5) situated this prophecy in 1730. Sattin, however, assigned it to 1727 and added that "M. du Lescoät seemed to declare to her that she would not be with her husband for long" (p. 11). Since we are dealing here with a prophecy, according to the authors we have quoted, it must have been made before François d'Youville's death. In 1727, the decline of the General Hospital was less evident than three years later, when the possibility of a change in administration would have had almost no prophetic quality.

determination to devote herself to serving her human brothers and sisters. It all began the mysterious day she understood "how truly God is a Father."

Chapter II

REMOTE PREPARATION

Marguerite's experience of 1727 was both the end of one road for her and the point of departure towards a new one. For a long time the "God of all goodness," [1] had been at work in her. One day she would marvel at His purposes. Lacking her own testimony, we must refer to historical data to ascertain the natural bases for this grace "which the Spirit of adoption would infuse into her soul and which would cause her to cry Abba, Father!" [2] Rather than destroying, grace brings to perfect fulfillment; it met with exceptional cooperation in her. This cooperation developed from the talents with which God blessed her, the influences which marked her and the experiences by which God opened new paths in her spirit.

It has been said that a child spontaneously attributes to God the qualities he admires in his own father. [3] Marguerite indirectly paid tribute to Christophe Dufrost de Lajemmerais the day she placed her destiny in the hands of God whose goodness had earlier been shown her through this

---

1. Mme d'Youville's letter to the abbé de l'Isle-Dieu, Sept. 21, 1771.
2. Pope John XXIII, Apostolic Letter, p. 3.
3. Babin, P., O.M.I., Dieu et l'adolescent, p. 63.

9

Breton gentleman and army officer. After his arrival in Canada in 1685, [4] he rapidly won the approval of his superiors. Several times, reports intended for the Ministry of the Navy mention his services and recommend his promotion. In 1705, Lajemmerais was made captain, the highest rank he could reach in the colonial army. He was an upright man, courageous and good, who knew how to create an atmosphere of love and of relative security in his home. The eldest of his children grew up in this climate. But this was a privilege which cost dearly when Lajemmerais died in 1708. Marguerite was then seven years old. More clearly than her brothers and sisters she could see the contrast in the life of their home before and after his death. Before, they were certainly poor but the captain's pay provided for the needs of the household. With the death of their father, poverty turned into such destitution that the governmental authorities were moved by it. Vaudreuil and Raudot announced to the Minister of the Navy that Captain Lajemmerais had died that summer. "He leaves a wife and six children in indigence. It is a pity to see this family so desolate and unable to provide for the future." [5] This appeal must have obtained scant result, for four years later the Governor reiterated his appeal for help. "Mesdames Puigibault[6] and

---

4. Champagne, A., Dictionnaire biographique canadien 2, p. 210. The details concerning Christophe Dufrost de Lajemmerais are found in his file in the Archives of the Grey Nuns in Montreal.

5. Bulletin des Recherches historiques, 1957, p. 292, letter of Nov. 4, 1708. Vaudreuil was governor general and Raudot, intendant.

6. Sister of Mme de Lajemmerais, aunt and god-mother of Marguerite.

Lajemmerais are in dire straits. They go on living only through the alms given to them." [7]

These contributions could not have been very substantial if we consider the poverty of the people of Varennes. It is therefore logical to conclude that Marguerite suffered from hunger and cold, and that she felt keenly the humiliation of living on charity. These experiences could have aroused bitterness and even revolt in her heart. Instead, they alerted her to the needs of others and helped her to understand that there is one thing no one allows to be violated — his human dignity. She would later remember that there are sufferings we do not want to admit, and that at times our way of helping others is like insulting them. Her exquisite courtesy to the poor goes back to those years when, reduced to the necessity of accepting charity, she learned how to give it. In this harsh school, Marguerite's pride encountered the first attack on it. At the same time, she precociously but confusedly associated in her mind the roles of provider and of father. We can understand that later the words 'Heavenly Father' and 'Divine Providence' meant the same Person to her. Since she was the object of the care of Divine Providence, the association of the two titles was that much easier for her at such an early age.

Providence is pleased to help men through other men. God inspired her great-grandfather, Pierre Boucher, to open his home to the eldest of the Lajemmerais family. [8] During the time she spent

7. Rapport de l'Archiviste de la prov. de Québec, 1947-48, p. 85; letter of Nov. 10, 1712.
8. Les Ursulines de Québec, vol. 2, p. 177: maternal great-grandfather of Marguerite, father of Marie who was the wife of René Gaultier de Varennes, grandfather of Marie-Renée who was the wife of Christophe Dufrost de Lajemmerais.

there, Marguerite personally came to know a just man, an exceptional father, a man of faith formed by that giant of the missions, Jean de Brébeuf, whose missionary work he had shared in the Huron territory. His teachings did not fall into barren ground. After reaching posts of command because of his reputation for personal bravery, Pierre Boucher freely gave them up to establish his estate at Iles Percées. To explain his action, he set forth a real program of life which gives the measure of the man. "I am leaving Three Rivers and will henceforth reside at my estate at Boucherville," he wrote "so there may be a place in this country consecrated to God; in order to live a retired life free of the confusion of the world; to work out my salvation and that of my family; to set aside some legitimate earnings to assure the support of my family; to develop a beautiful land which I hold from God; and to help the poor." [9]

The founder of Boucherville never wavered in this program. He was the father of fifteen children, three of whom entered religious life. He was a father to the tenant farmers whom he helped in all kinds of circumstances. He was a father to the poor who never appealed to his goodness in vain. Despite his eighty-six years, Pierre Boucher did not hesitate to hold out a helping hand to the Lajemmerais family. So he offered to Marguerite not only house and home but also the privilege of an initiation into real values — domestic and social virtues and especially the greatest commandment — love. Her great-grandfather earnestly stated in his will: "To you, my dear children, I recommend peace, harmony, and unity among yourselves. Never allow selfish interests to create the

9. These reasons are reproduced in their entirety in Mitchell, E. *Messire Pierre Boucher*, p. 156 ff.

least division among you...love one another and do everything in the sight of God."

Unity, charity, almsgiving are recommendations which recur constantly in the advice he gave his children. He especially urged them to place their trust in God and to give themselves into His hands. "Trust in His goodness and He will give you what you need. Live in the fear of the Lord and He will take care of you." And to his daughter, Louise, who refused many advantageous opportunities to help her parents, he said, "God will take care of you and be a father to you!" [10]

This encouragement was engraved in Marguerite's soul and she saw it fulfilled before her eyes. The daily bread she had learned to ask from "Our Father" she received through Pierre Boucher — material bread, necessary for life; the bread of affection because she was an orphan; and the spiritual bread which drew her towards God the Father. This teaching of Pierre Boucher continued beyond his death since it became a custom of his descendants "to read his last will" on their knees on each anniversary of his death. [11]

This text would take on a special significance in 1727 when "it pleased God" [12] to open her mind to the mystery of love. She would find there the basis for her meditation as her own spiritual will and testament would show. Later, during her years of married solitude, she would have time to reflect on

---

10. Mitchell E. op. cit., p. 341 ff.
11. P. Boucher died April 19, 1717 at ninety-five years of age. Marguerite was then fifteen years old.
12. This expression recurs six times in Marguerite's correspondence.

her life. And she would realize that the time spent at Boucherville had marked in a way the first stage of her journey towards God. May we not discern an implicit allusion to those childhood years when she would cry out ecstatically at the limitless resources of Providence " We are always on the verge of lacking everything yet we never lack what we need." [13] As an orphan she would have had nothing if her great grandfather had not carried out the commandment he gave to his family: "Give alms as much as you can." [14]

Marguerite was indebted to Pierre Boucher for another benefit. Thanks to his influence, she was admitted as a student in the Ursuline Convent in Quebec in August, 1712. Forty years had gone by since the death of Marie of the Incarnation, but the influence and reputation of this great mystic had outlived her. Through the teaching of the Ursulines, the adolescent Marguerite discovered the road that leads to the Heavenly Father. "There is no way to come to the Father except by passing through the gate (Jn 10:9) which leads to Him and which is His most adorable Son," wrote Marie of the Incarnation to her friends. [15] Fifteen years later, she synthetized her teaching for Dom Claude Martin, her son, in the famous apostolic prayer: "Through the heart of Jesus, my way, my truth, my life, I draw near to you, O Eternal Father." [16] And the famous missionary, faithful to her charism, "made a (spiritual) trip around the world searching for souls to offer them to the

---

13. Letter to the abbé de l'Isle-Dieu, Sept. 22, 1770.
14. Mitchell, E. op. cit., p. 344.
15. Letter of Oct. 7, 1646.
16. Letter of Sept. 16, 1661. The prayer was recited daily in the convent.

Father through the heart of His Son." Going to the Father through the beloved Son, the gift of His Providence, drawing from His heart the love with which to love God and her human brothers and sisters — these are characteristics we find later in the life and writings of Marguerite, proof of the spiritual relationship which links her to the "Teresa of the New World." [17]

In the convent at Quebec, this adolescent girl's personality revealed itself — a quick mind, discerning judgment, [18] and a sense of responsibility. When she declined to participate in her classmates' games she would explain: "These girls are more fortunate than I. For my part, I must hurry to learn in order to help my mother at home." [19] Such attitudes in so young a child did not escape Mother Mary of the Angels, the superior, who was responsible for teaching Christian Doctrine whenever a teacher had to be replaced. [20] She was a good psychologist; fifty-three years of religious life had familiarized her with God's ways. She sensed that a great destiny awaited this student who had already begun to walk along the royal road of trials. And that is probably why she gave her the

---

17. Jamet, Dom A.: *Le témoignage de Marie de l'Incarnation*, p. 342. Marguerite most probably read the life of Marie de l'Incarnation by Claude Martin. This had been in circulation in the convent since 1677 and the nuns urged others to read it. (Emmanuel, Sr.: *Marie de l'Incarnation in her letters*, p. 226, note 37).

18. Sr. Marie de l'Assomption, O.S.U. to Mother Deschamps, S.G.M. Dec. 10, 1895.

19. Words reported by oral tradition.

20. AMDG. Histoire des Ursulines, p. 122.

book entitled *The Holy Ways of the Cross* by Henri-Marie Boudon, Canon of Evreux. [21] The book was not easy to understand but this fine teacher felt that one day Mademoiselle de Lajemmerais would understand its meaning.

Truly, she would grasp its meaning, but there would be no short cuts for Marguerite in following the way prepared for her by Providence. She would first have to "suffer without any consolation and shed very bitter tears." The proof that she then consulted *The Holy Ways of the Cross* can be ascertained from the fact that we know from whom she obtained the book. This is, then, probably derived from a statement of Madame d'Youville herself. Further, once her vocation had become clearer, she ordered other copies of the book from France, thus indicating that she had absorbed the teachings of abbé Boudon: "The cross is love's tool with which the Father of mercies works in those He chooses, to conform them to His Son."

Nevertheless, she could not foresee the influence this small book would have on the development of her understanding. At the end of the summer of 1714, she returned to the half-timber house on the banks of the St. Lawrence. Her younger brothers and sisters, obviously impressed at the sight of this tall young girl, noted that "although she was twelve years old, she seemed to be fifteen." [22] Fortunately they did not limit themselves to this physical description. From their testimony we can sketch the

---

21. See Longpré, A. *"L'influence spirituelle de Boudon"* in Revue d'Histoire de l'Amérique française, v. III, p. 203.

22. Dufrost, Ist manuscript, p. 2. When she returned from Québec, Marguerite was completing her thirteenth year.

psychological portrait of the woman she would become. Willingness to work, fortitude, were evident in this eldest daughter who was still quite young and who was suddenly to become her mother's confidante and helper and, at the same time, the teacher of her brothers and sisters.

In addition to supporting the household by her work as a seamstress and embroiderer, Marguerite also grew accustomed to exercising authority. Learning to govern means learning to serve; to require the accomplishment of a task or duty means committing oneself to accomplish it. And to win trust one must first deserve it. So the budding teacher trained herself by forming her clear-sighted pupils, observers of her daily life. Tact, psychological insight, availability, respect for others, self-forgetfulness, the spirit of sharing — these were the attitudes the young girl had to acquire or develop. Success crowned her efforts. "Marguerite," her younger brothers and sisters found, "knows how to be feared and to be loved." To be loved, especially, for she inspired in them an "extraordinary attachment" in return for the "truly tender affection" she poured out on them. Still more, she became the "confidante of their secrets." [23]

She did not pretend to be an angel, however. "The world held attractions for her. She loved good company and the enjoyments of life; she shared the weakness of young persons of her sex who love to look beautiful and to be loved." [24] So Marguerite was a genuine young girl, eager to find her place in the world. And the world seemed to smile on her. Poverty was no stumbling-block. The reputation of

---

23. Dufrost, Ist manuscript, pp. 2 & 3.
24. Ibid., p. 4.

the Boucher family, the nobility of the name Dufrost de Lajemmerais since 1409 [25] were joined in her to physical beauty: chiseled features, an expressive gaze, a ruddy complexion and a queenly bearing. "A very advantageous and very honorable suitor presented himself." According to tradition, M. de Langloiserie was the name of the suitor who courted Mlle de Lajemmerais; everything seemed to point to a happy marriage. But the young girl's mother eloped with Timothy Sullivan-Sylvain, a questionable character who succeeded in ingratiating himself with Vaudreuil [26] and ended up by obtaining a license to practice medicine in Montreal. This unfortunate marriage put an end to Langloiserie's attentions. Wounded in her love and in her filial affection as well as in her pride, Marguerite saw her dream fade away. We can hardly doubt that she shuddered under this humiliating blow. "Very few persons, however, would know of this cross," according to her son, Charles. It was a cross caused, at least partly by "a person who was closely related to her by blood." [27]

Marguerite's reaction to this abandonment was to overcome her sadness, proving her strength of character, and to keep hoping in the future. She expected to find happiness at last the day she joined her life to that of François d'Youville. [28] This would not be a happiness achieved once and for all but a

---

25. Roy, P.-G., Bulletin des Recherches historiques, 1920, v. 2, pp. 71-77.

26. Fauteux, A., Bulletin des Recherches historiques, Nov. 1917, p. 335. Sylvain, who had a quarrelsome streak, was frequently in trouble with the courts. But, according to Mme de Vaudreuil, "he acted like a father to the Lajemmerais children".

27. Dufrost, 2nd manuscript, p. 27.

28. August, 12, 1722.

happiness to be won, created day after day by mutual adaptation, by mutual acceptance of sacrifice. "Crosses there must be," she would write later of married life, "but love makes us strong enough to bear them." [29] Love, union — to her it was the same thing. And Marguerite was unaccountably deprived of them. She would have to decide whether to give up hope or to go beyond it, taking on the burden of loving without return, like the God "who first loved us." (Jn. 4:19) God's grace in her life encouraged Marguerite to choose love.

---

29. Letter to M. et Mme de Figuery, Aug. 20, 1766.

Chapter III

LOVE IS GIFT

Marguerite's choice did not grant her immunity from suffering any more than it freed her from the unhappiness inherent in the human condition. Gradually God's plan for her would emerge in the apparent paradox of a call to great holiness and a humanly tragic situation. To her, only one certainty was clear: she knew that she was the object of God's eternal love. On this infinite love her desire was focused. But this desire concealed a danger. She might try to escape from the daily drabness of life under the pretext of opening herself more completely to God. With a very sure sense of spiritual realities, she avoided this trap. She looked for God in the simplicity of her heart [1] and discovered Him where He lets us find Him — in the day's work. "A masculine mind, a solid judgment," her son would say. She took advantage of the means at hand, choosing reality rather than illusion.

At this time the work of preparation for her future vocation took place. For meditation her director suggested to her the attitudes of Jesus and Mary toward the Eternal Father. [2] *The Holy Ways of the Cross* taught her that "no one was loved more by the

---

1. Dufrost, 1st manuscript, p. 6.
2. Faillon, E.-M., *Vie de M. Olier*, v. 3, pp. 70-72.

Father than Jesus, and no one suffered so much." [3] Finally, the Confraternity of the Holy Family which she joined in 1727, [4] probably on M. du Lescoät's advice, proposed the duty of imitating the Virgin in whom and through whom great things were accomplished. The diversity of these suggestions was only an apparent one. Looking at them more closely, we can appreciate their unity since everything ultimately contributed to centering one's effort on a single objective: to see in God "the Father who so loved the world that He gave His only Son" (Jn. 3:16) born of a woman blessed among all women.

Marguerite saw the source of Mary's greatness in her divine motherhood. This woman was chosen by God Himself to give the world His beloved Son, the gift of Divine Providence. By living intimately with her, by praying in union with her, she came to understand this mystery of faith more and more deeply. One day she would express her complete realization by invoking Mary under the title of Our Lady of Providence. In the light of the grace of her conversion, everything is expressed in the love of the Father Who foresaw the needs of humanity and provided for them.

It would be fruitless to look for texts in which Marguerite described her devotion to Mary. Here again, her acts revealed her thoughts. When she pronounced private vows, she knelt at the feet of Our Lady of Providence [5] to learn from her how to give God to others. To the Virgin of the Presentation she confided the ministry she began on November 21,

---

3. Boudon, op. cit., p. 41.

4. Angers, p. 346, note 11.

5. The small Statue of the Virgin and Child was given to Mme d'Youville by a priest. (Dufrost, 1st manuscript, p. 7).

1737. Through her intercession she also prayed for the cure of her work's protector, M. Normant. [6] On the day after the devastating fire of 1745, she vowed herself to total poverty under the protection of Our Lady of the Purification. [7] And two years after assuming the administration of the General Hospital, she would obtain a plenary indulgence for the feast of the Annunciation. [8] Finally, when her last moments had come, she would ask Our Lady of Providence to watch over her death. [9] This final prayer, after so many others, proves that as a member of the Confraternity of the Holy Family, she had learned to go to Mary for help in every situation.

"How would the Virgin act in this situation?" The handbook of the Confraternity recommended this question as a way of leading its married members to model their lives on Mary's. [10] This practice combines action and contemplation — action inspired by contemplation whose authenticity it reveals. Marguerite adopted this directive. So we should not be surprised at the balanced, the realistic attitude she displayed in her search for God. "Her devotion is solid, unaffected, not at all austere or remarkable," declared abbé Charles Dufrost, her son, who was a witness of his mother's prudence. [11] Like Mary, Marguerite kept the memory of God's special moment of

---

6. "First she prayed to the Eternal Father, promising to order a painting of Him from France and also to burn a candle before the Blessed Sacrament in the parish church on the feast of the Presentation". (Faillon, pp. 43-44).

7. Original Commitment, signed Feb. 2, 1745.

8. Faillon, p. 274.

9. Mother Deschamps to Mme J.-J. Girouard, Sept. 7, 1855.

10. *The Catechism of true Devotion*, p. 26.

11. Dufrost, 1st manuscript, pp. 5-6.

grace in her heart. This experience transformed her view of life and gave a new meaning to it. And the "wonderful exchange" which continued from then on took place in the secrecy of her soul. In return for what she offered, she received an overflowing measure of love, for the Holy Spirit prepared her to be the means of pouring out this love.

Mme d'Youville waged her first campaign against François, the unfortunate husband who kept pretending to be a great man. What a painful contrast between the man who drained the cup of empty pleasure to the dregs and the woman who welcomed him when he returned home. It was humiliating for the proud Marguerite to see herself relegated to the background in the concerns of her fickle husband. But her love was not deadened; it was sublimated and gave itself freely. In her eyes, the sufferings she kept to herself, the tenderness with which she surrounded François constituted the means of redeeming an immortal soul she wanted to save.

Finally, in June 1730, the day came when the Sieur de la Découverte entered his home for the last time. He returned to die, stricken down by false pleurisy, [12] victim of his pursuit of pleasure. Who could describe the concern of his nurse, on duty day and night next to the bed where he fought for his life. He was the object of a love which had not failed since the wedding vows of August 12, 1722. During his lifetime, he had ignored that love, but it must have been good for him to see her standing at his

---

12. Oral tradition recounts that François d'Youville may have been wounded by an Indian's arrow. There is no supporting documentation, but this is still plausible if we take into account the contemptible dealings of the fur-trader with the Nipissing Indians at Ile-aux-Tourtes.

bedside at the moment of death. Who can say? Perhaps the hope of the Creator's mercy was reborn in him at the sight of such merciful love at his service. After having been the principal source of Marguerite's sufferings, her husband became the object of her "revenge". But revenge — for those who aim at holiness — is like God's revenge: overflowing forgiveness where sin abounds.

Once death had completed its work, Francois' body was buried and Mme d'Youville paid the stipend for three hundred sixty requiem Masses [13] for the man who left her with two living children, a third child who would be born in February, 1731, a considerable inheritance of debts, [14] and sad memories. Once again, Marguerite did not react according to human expectations. "The indifference and harshness of her husband did not keep her from being greatly afflicted by his death; she wept a great deal for him for a long time." [15] Not long ago Marguerite had wept other, bitter tears because of him. These were now turned into prayers that God would welcome into his peace the soul of François You, Sieur de la Découverte, deceased in the thirtieth year of his life, July 4, 1730.

A chapter in Mme d'Youville's life was closed. What events would mark the new period which was just beginning? The future unveils its mystery only dimly. Soon ceaseless toil would claim her — the means of support for herself and her children. Soon too, the desire to give herself completely into God's

---

13. Inventory of François d'Youville's possessions, Angers, p. 187.

14. Dufrost, 2nd manuscript, p. 4. Charles was born July 18, 1729. Ignace, the posthumous child, would be born Feb. 26, 1731 and would die July 17 of that year.

15. Dufrost, 1st manuscript, p. 5.

hands would grow in her. Not in vain had she been given her special grace. On October 23, 1731, she became a member of the Confraternity of the Heart of Jesus and was enrolled in the membership at the monastery in Quebec. Wordlessly, without fanfare, she indicated by this significant act that through the prayer of her adolescence she had found the only way leading to the Father.

The Spirit had formed this servant. She was now ready for action. Marguerite would herself be amazed one day "that He condescends to use such a poor person to bring about some small good." [16]

---

16. Letter to the abbé de l'Isle-Dieu, Sept. 22, 1770.

Chapter IV

TOWARDS HUMAN BROTHERHOOD

It may have been relatively easy to look for God in the solitude of a joyless home. But continuing this search immersed in overwhelming activity undoubtedly demands continually renewed effort. For this reason it points to a strong motivation. Marguerite's son, Charles, saw this clearly. To convey his admiration to his readers, he gave a detailed account of Mme d'Youville's daily schedule.

"After the death of her husband, seeing herself without money or other resources, she decided to open a small shop to support herself and her children. Having found friends who gave her merchandise on credit, she went to live in a house near the square in the lower town, believing that this was a better location for a business. [1] Her piety had grown since she had become a widow; bad weather could not prevent her from attending Mass daily and, in the afternoon, from going to adore the Blessed Sacrament when her occupations allowed her to do so... From the very first years of her widowhood, she was filled with charity for her neighbor and considered it a duty

1. A notarized deed, dated Sept. 14, 1730, proves that this house was located on the rue du St-Sacrement. Mme d'Youville would probably return to the Place du Marché when this house was awarded to her legally Oct. 31, 1732. (Archives judiciaires de Montréal, registre 14 des audiences, p. 168).

and an honor to visit the poor, the sick, the prisoners, taking from what she needed herself to ease the sufferings of Christ's members. People were edified to see her, going from door to door, begging for what she needed to bury criminals... visiting the poor in the city hospital and mending the ragged clothing of the destitute." [2]

This long enumeration, is, however, incomplete. The priest fails to mention the hearings needed to settle François d'Youville's estate and the other difficulties the young widow had to face. For not everyone she encountered was her friend; and, in her struggle to go on, she was forced to defend herself against false claims. Justice and prudence are difficult virtues to practice, so doubtless, in particularly delicate matters, Marguerite asked advice of more experienced persons, as her later correspondence indicates. She defended her rights gently but firmly, and she needed to be firm in order to prevent herself from being swindled and giving in to the lure of success. Success was to be hers. Here again her son did not pause to reflect that this was a special kind of success. Nor did he attribute it to her exceptional gifts. Twice he declared that "she was not a rare and brilliant mind." [3] This opinion is contested somewhat by M. Montgolfier who praised "the uncommon intelligence of Mme d'Youville". [4] Eminent historians went so far as to call her a woman of genius [5] and her companions would be amazed

---

2. Dufrost, 1st manuscript, pp. 5-6.

3. Ibid., p. 2.

4. Montgolfier, Constitutions, p. 44. Montgolfier who arrived in Montreal in 1751 observed her intelligence in action.

5. Groulx, Ch. L.: *Une femme de génie au Canada.*

at the success of her undertakings [6] which they would attribute to her confidence in Providence. [7] Her biographer, Faillon, declared that in his opinion, the first effect of the grace she had received in 1727 was "to inspire in her the means of earning her living," and, in further statements, he agreed with Charles Dufrost that it was "to satisfy her great love for the unfortunate." [8]

Cares and worries provided her with many opportunities to realize that "the closer we come to God, the more clearly we see into temporal affairs." [9] Business matters did not close her heart to other people's needs. In this period, perhaps the most insecure of her life, she found ways of helping the poor and the unfortunate who surrounded her. As a needy widow, should she not have been satisfied with providing for her own needs! How can we explain this zeal which was so contrary to realistic human prudence, unless we say that Marguerite preferred to follow the teachings of divine wisdom? What did she gain from this extra effort except overwork? According to some people, she made herself ridiculous; and the members of her own family did not hide their disapproval. [10]

Mme d'Youville left her life as the detailed account of the growth of her thoughts and desires. By contemplating God as Father of all men, she came to realize that men are truly brothers. She grasped the implications of the Gospel commandment: "What

---

6. Sattin, p. 11.

7. Dufrost, 2nd manuscript, p. 24.

8. Faillon, pp. 19-20.

9. Words of Marie de l'Incarnation to one of her sisters, Sept. 3, 1645.

10. Dufrost, 1st manuscript, p. 8.

you have done to one of these, the least of my brothers, you have done to me." Heartfelt kindness, concern for others, the spirit of sharing, the gifts of nature and grace — all these the Spirit gradually taught her, guiding her toward a new stage in her spiritual growth. Her own difficulties kept her alert, making it easy for her to subsitute herself for the needy, thus able to sympathize with their misfortune. The handbook of devotion to the Holy Family taught her to give to others in spite of her own poverty. "If you have little, give little; if you have a great deal, give much; whatever you give, give it willingly. Could the Master possibly abandon those who obey his commands for love of Him!" [11] Strengthened by this assurance, the young widow found a solution to her dilemma. Since she had little material goods, she gave herself, "considering it a duty and an honor to visit the poor, the sick, the prisoners," offering to some what help she could, and to others the message of hope and trust in God. She became a social worker, arriving unexpectedly, as though by accident, to lend a helping hand. And she did this without neglecting her own responsibilities. "She was not one of those women who neglect their own homes and the needs of their children and servants," her son Charles pointed out. [12] When the poverty

---

11. *Recueil de la vraie dévotion*, p. 185.

12. Dufrost, 1st manuscript, p. 6. It is impossible to ascertain whether Mme d'Youville had servants at this time. The inventory of the estate drawn up in April, 1731, mentions a Pawnee slave about 10 or 11 years old, valued at 150 pounds! "In Canada, slaves were either Negroes or Indians captured in war or bought from the Five Nations by the French". "These slaves were in the service of various individuals or institutions and led a relatively happy life". Slavery was not abolished in Canada until 1833 by a law of Parliament". (Champagne, A.: *Les La Vérendrye et le Poste de l'Ouest*, pp. 358-359).

she encountered was too great, "she took from what she herself needed to provide for the poor." The necessities of life, of which François' negligence had deprived her, she now sacrificed in favor of those poorer than herself. Who can doubt that she gave joyfully when she freely chose to find her happiness in concern for the happiness of others! Some people were shocked by these activities: but, on the other hand, there were those who understood. Mme d'Youville was elected a member of the council of the Confraternity of the Holy Family on June 5, 1731, less than a year after François' death. [13] This association, whose rule was like that of a religious order, required a great deal of its members and especially of its officers. Marguerite's election, which was an unqualified vote of confidence, was also a tacit approval of her charitable activities.

Had she found a way of life which was authentically hers? Considering the obligations she had assumed and the extra work she imposed on herself, we could say that God had his rightful place in her life. But one desire still haunted her — to do still more, to fill her cup to the brim. For her, loving meant acting; loving truly meant loving selflessly, imitating Divine Providence which responds before we ask. It meant being at the service of Providence like a hand distributing gifts and graces; it meant making visible the care of the Heavenly Father for his children. This was the ideal found in the life of Christ which she admired and wanted to follow. So it is not surprising to see her move progressively toward the life work which would soon claim all her energy.

---

13. Angers, p. 346, note 11.

When she enrolled in the Confraternity of the Blessed Sacrament in 1733, another good work was suggested to her: "obtaining a proper burial for criminals and outcasts." [14] "Begging from door to door" was awkward for her; and until then she had refused to do so, even in exceptionally difficult situations. This would always be repugnant to her independent spirit. Twenty years later she would inform colonial authorities that she did not count on the contributions of the French court to support the General Hospital. [15] "Providence and our work are the resources on which we depend," she would write to the same authorities two years later. [16] We may sense a hint of pride in these words, even though she had already been the object of many a snub. For Mme d'Youville as for every one else, humility was not an easy virtue to learn. But as love took root and grew in her, light was given her to see that she was a "poor person" called by God to "bring about some good." A day would come (now in the distant future), when, confronted with a direct intervention of Providence, she would exclaim, "Heavens, I am a wretched creature!" [17] Meanwhile, she continued her struggle and contemplated Christ humiliated in His Passion. For her annual hour of adoration before the Blessed Sacrament, she chose three o'clock on Good Friday. [18] The Eucharist would deepen her understanding of the

---

14. Règlement de l'Adoration perpétuelle du St-Sacrement et de la bonne Mort, typewritten text, p. 4. Mme d'Youville joined the Association, March 16, 1733.

15. Petition of Mme d'Youville and her companions, 1750.

16. Report of June 19, 1752.

17. Sattin, p. 44. The incident is said to have occurred in 1766.

18. Furthermore, the Association required a weekly half-hour of adoration.

cross and would spur her on never to balk before works requiring the destruction of self-love. So the proud Marguerite held out a begging hand, meeting contributions and refusals, learning the art of self-renunciation through these rejections. Providence favored her efforts. In 1734,[19] she was named directress of postulants in the Confraternity of the Holy Family, and was urged "to surpass the other members in fervor, watchfulness and humility." [20] Further, she was expected to teach the candidates how to live in the spirit of the Holy Family.

Marguerite's preparation for teaching had been limited to the experience she had had in her home at Varennes, and more recently, with her children. How, then, did she fulfill this position as teacher of spirituality, since this was really her role? M. H.-F. Gravé, director of the seminary of Quebec, went so far as to praise "this teacher whose worth is so far beyond the ordinary." [21] And the Grey Nuns who would later benefit from her teaching would say: "We delighted in gathering around her, seated at her feet; and there we experienced every kind of joy at hearing her speak with us." [22]

Mme d'Youville found her teachings in the booklet on True Devotion and especially in what the Master "who speaks without need of words, without clash of opinions, without display and without

---

19. She was re-elected to this position five times, indicating that she fulfilled its duties to the satisfaction of the members.
20. La solide dévotion, p. 39, art. VIII.
21. Letter to Mother Despins, Jan. 5, 1772. Obliged to flee from Quebec in 1759, M. Gravé remained in Montreal until 1761, during which time he assumed the chaplaincy of the General Hospital.
22. Sattin, p. 36.

arguments", [23] had revealed to her. Marguerite discovered God's purpose for her own life as she entered more deeply into the life of the Holy Family. Setting aside a major portion of her life for the Lord was no longer enough for her. She wanted to consecrate her whole being to Him in religious life. This life consistent with her charism of "sharing in God's Fatherhood" [24] would be a life of "childlike intimacy with the Heavenly Father" [25] and it would express, through the works of mercy, God's tender love for his earthly sons and daughters.

23. *Imitation of Christ*, Book III, ch. XLIII. This was a bedside book for Mme d'Youville. Reading from it was imposed by rule of the community.

24. Faillon, p. 268.

25. Philipon, P. M.-M., o.p.: *Le portrait spirituel de Mère d'Youville*, Dec. 12, 1959.

Chapter V

THE CRY OF THOSE WHO SUFFER

It would be a mistake to think that God's call to total detachment suppresses all resistance in the human heart. God offers Himself; He does not impose himself. "He stands at the door and knocks," (Rev. 3:20). He does not force the door but waits for it to open of itself. Probably the prospect of leaving a way of life in which it was possibble for her to do some good in order to launch into the unknown frightened Marguerite, even if, as usual, she did not openly express her feelings. Probably she experienced the temptation to refuse, to turn aside at the approach of the cross. God's grace would prove stronger than her weakness, however. She asked the advice of the superior of the Seminary, M. Normant, [1] whom she had chosen as her director after the death of M. du Lescoät. [2]

"One cannot say whether M. Normant, a truly priestly man of wise judgment and great prudence, suggested to her that she consecrate herself to the service of the poor; or whether she herself told him of her desire to establish a community of women,"

---

1. Louis Normant du Faradon was born in May, 1681 and entered the Sulpicians, Nov. 2, 1706. He arrived in Canada in 1722 and was bursar and then superior of the Seminary from 1732 until June 18, 1759, the date of his death.
2. February 7, 1733.

declared her contemporaries. [3] One thing is certain. M. Normant advised her "to take some poor people in to live with her and to try out what she would one day make a reality. [4]

She hoped to bring about the establishment of a community of religious women in the Canadian colony while the Court of France formally prohibited a foundation. [5] To realize this project while her two children were still young and had only herself for support presented a difficulty which of itself would justify Marguerite's hesitation. Furthermore, the foundation of a community required willing collaborators. The Lord provided for this need.

Mme d'Youville found a rare friend in Mlle Louise Thaumur de la Source. [6] This was a recent friendship, begun early in 1737. Marguerite instinctively knew, however, that Louise would be the ideal companion to join her in founding this association of lay women dedicated to the relief of the poor. If the court would not consent to the forming of a new community, then they would form a group of lay volunteers, counting only on the resources of Providence and their own work for their support and for the care of the poor.

The time came for the final decision. Marguerite had refrained from telling her plans to her friend,

3. Dufrost, 1st manuscript, p. 7; Sattin, p. 12.

4. Faillon, p. 31. M. Normant, who saw the decay of the General Hospital, suspected that Mme d'Youville would be the individual prepared by the Lord to prevent its total ruin. (p. 30).

5. Frégault, G., *Le XVIIIè siècle canadien*, p. 117.

6. She was the daughter of Dominique Thaumur de la Source, a surgeon of the Hôtel-Dieu and of Jeanne Prud'homme. One of her brothers was a priest and one of her sisters was a member of the Congregation of Notre-Dame.

for she did not want friendship to play a part in Mlle de la Source's decision. This respect for others' freedom would largely explain Mme d'Youville's future success as a foundress. She was convinced that only the Holy Spirit can bring about the will to do good and its accomplishment. So she merely suggested to her companion that they make a retreat and a novena at the grave of M. du Lescoät, to discern "what they could both do for the glory of God." [7] Through the intercession of this guide who had led her in the way of confidence and abandonment to the heavenly Father, Marguerite prayed for the courage and strength needed to accomplish her purpose. [8]

Once the retreat was over, the two friends went to the Seminary where M. Normant "exhorted them in very inspiring words about the happiness of those who serve Jesus Christ in the person of the poor." [9] More than once, during her charitable excursions, Marguerite had experienced the happiness M. Normant pointed out. She must have seen changes simply because of her presence. A small attention, a smile, an alms, a service rendered was enough to strengthen a wavering courage, to enliven a dying faith — all because it is easier to believe in God's merciful love expressed in tireless human goodness. She freely gave hope and courage, goods that the most precious gold could not buy, to the point of being caught in this marvelous and magnanimous game of love, not suspecting that one day the Master would ask still more of her. Until now, she had served others because of God, but without giving

7. Sattin, p. 12.
8. This retreat must have taken place towards the end of the summer, since the lease for the LeVerrier house was dated Sept. 28, 1737.
9. Sattin, p. 12.

up her freedom. Henceforth, she would reach God through her brothers and sisters in need. The simple comfort earned by honest work which finally allowed her to know a relative security seemed unacceptable to her as long as the poor and needy suffered around her. Marguerite decided to put her plans into action and confided her decision to Mlle de la Source who first expressed surprise and indecision but then agreed wholeheartedly with her friend's proposal.

Two other companions, Catherine Cusson and Catherine Demers, [10] probably guided also by M. Normant, came to offer their help. It would seem that the associates lived together under the same roof [11] while waiting to move into the LeVerrier house which they leased September 28, 1737. [12] The possessions of these lay women "which were worth no more than one hundred pistoles" according to Charles Dufrost were transported surreptitiously to the new home on the vigil of All Saints' Day. There, in a room set aside as an oratory, they placed the copper statuette of the Virgin and Child, gift of a priest, in the place of honor. Upon entering, they set

10. Catherine Cusson, the daughter of Jean and Marguerite Aubuchon, was born in 1709. Orphaned in early childhood, she lived with her two sisters. All three supported themselves by sewing. Catherine Demers, daughter of Robert Demers, a tailor, and Magdeleine Jetté, was the eldest of the group. (Archives of the Grey Nuns of Montreal, files of Sisters Cusson and Demers).

11. This could not be the house on the Place du Marché which had been sold at auction in 1735 to settle the estate of the La Découverte family. (Angers, A.-F., Report entitled: Maisons habitées ou fréquentées par Mme d'Youville, in the Archives of the Grey Nuns).

12. The lease was to take effect Oct. 1, 1737. The addition of some bedrooms on the 3rd floor postponed their occupancy until Oct. 31. (Sattin, p. 14).

a precedent; they knelt at the feet of Our Lady of
Providence. In her own name and in the name of her
companions, Mme d'Youville "begged the Virgin to
look favorably on the little society whose only intention was to consecrate themselves forever to the
service of the poor." The ideal she expressed must
have been beautiful, for Sister Lasource and Sister
Cusson listened in tears. Like Marguerite, Sister
Demers showed no external signs of emotion. Soon
M. Normant arrived and spoke to them, this time
not only of the timeliness of the undertaking but
also of the persecutions it would arouse.

A small, eight-year old boy watched this event
take place. He did not understand its meaning then;
but later, when he recounted it, he would seize the
opportunity to point out the wisdom of his mother.
"To abandon her children in order to care for the
poor would have been the fruit of a badly conceived
devotion. Her love for the poor and her tenderness
for her children led her to find a way to devote herself
both to the poor and to her children," he wrote, [13]
recalling that distant day when he saw the community
of lay women begin.

The members set off, burning their bridges behind them, to make a return impossible. Henceforth,
they would walk together in the path of love of God
and charity for the poor. But it was important for them
to state precisely the life-style they wanted to adopt
in order to remain sensitive to the Lord and to keep
themselves available to those in whom He continues
to live.

---

13. Dufrost, 1st manuscript, p. 7. François, the older, entered the
Seminary in Quebec in 1737. Charles was still in the Sulpicians'
school in Montreal.

The loose-leaf sheets which constitute the first official document setting forth the purpose of the little society were "agreed upon by Mme d'Youville and her first companions, drawn up by M. Normant and originally written in his own hand." [14] It was consistent with her personality for Marguerite to ask for her companions' help in writing up this rule of life... Still it is true that her collaborators willingly learned from her; all three of them saw in her the initiator of their work and spontaneously they called her "Mother". [15] Should she not be the one to sketch the character portrait of the servant of the poor, specifying the hours of prayer, work and rest which favored a balanced life and the exercise of a demanding ministry? So we can see in these pages [16] the inner life of Mme d'Youville and the progress she had made since the grace she had received ten years earlier. She recommended the very means she herself used to unite her soul with God.

She did not minimize the demands of holiness, recommending total poverty, deep humility, complete obedience, childlike simplicity, irreproachable purity, continual mortification and limitless charity. "With a delicate conscience, she did not see evil everywhere," [17] but she was not unaware of its reality.

---

14. Montgolfier, Constitutions, p. 59. In the Archives of the Grey Nuns of Montreal are two original documents entitled: Rule. The first seems to be an outline which was tried out and then rewritten with some changes in the daily horarium and adopted, according to Sattin, some months after they moved to the new house.

15. Sattin, p. 15.

16. These loose leaf sheets are divided into two parts and include the daily schedule of times of prayer and the attitudes with which one should act. This latter is a commentary on the Rule itself. The full texts are given in the appendix.

17. Dufrost, 1st manuscript, p. 6.

Hence a warning against too great familiarity, against unfavorable relationships, of the danger of excessive visiting and social life, a vanity in dress which should be simple and modest. We can admire her human insight so evident in this rule of life where the Sisters are told "to make known one's needs, not hiding one's weaknesses, undertaking nothing which could injure one's health" and — for future postulants — in the total freedom they would have to withdraw after an honest attempt at this way of life.

The Foundress had no illusions about the instability of the human heart. She knew that laziness, boredom, discouragement can follow the most beautiful moments of enthusiasm. In the effort of daily self-giving, only an ever growing love can sustain one's courage. So she twice recommended prayer to Jesus and Mary, the Sisters' models, at five o'clock, the time for rising. The day was to be one of real prayer, beginning with this morning prayer, followed by a half-hour of contemplation, Mass and the reception of Holy Communion "on the days appointed." [18] During the day, two periods of spiritual reading, the particular examen, a visit to the Blessed Sacrament, the recitation of the rosary and of the Office of the Holy Name of Mary, and finally evening prayer would give rhythm to the work. Here the servants of the poor would draw from the hearts of Jesus and Mary the love they needed in order to love God and those they served for His sake. At the time of prayer they should "offer themselves to the Father with Jesus"; and at work, they should "see in the poor, the Christ whose members they have the honor to be."

---

18. Each Sister received Holy Communion three times a week and a fourth time in turn.

They would find their joy in the realization that they were helping the children of God and in the "perfect union" joining hearts and minds in the pursuit of the same ideal. Although they could not form a new community — they were forbidden to discuss anything relating to such a project — they were to behave as though they really were religious especially "in their interior dispositions." They did not adopt any special dress except for a belt of black material worn "over their dresses of ordinary dark-colored material".

This group of "lay women in dress but religious at heart" was to survive despite the opposition they foresaw. It had a promise of enduring life in the words of Christ Who said: "Indeed the poor you will always have with you" (Jn 12:18). How important was legal recognition when the members of the society had their place in the Church?

On November 21, 1737, the hospice welcomed its first guest — Françoise Auzon, a blind woman, whose husband, Pierre Lebeuf, would find a home in the Charon Brothers' hospital. [19] Nothing in this semi-official ceremony was left to chance or to the vagaries of circumstance. Mme d'Youville wished to offer her work to the Eternal Father on the day when the Blessed Virgin was presented in the temple. She did not mention it, but her work began as an act of forgiveness. The Lebeuf family had previously been engaged in the fur trade with her father-in-law [20] and had probably continued it with his sons.

By opening her doors to needy women, Marguerite was responding to a pressing need. There was

---

19. List of admissions, General Hospital, 1738.
20. Notarized list, vol. 2, p. 571. A copy is found in the Burton Collection, Detroit Public Library.

no provision for them in Montreal, for the General Hospital cared only for old men and orphans. Four poor women followed soon after Françoise Auzon, for their presence in the LeVerrier house on December 24 is noted. [21] And when December 31, 1737 came, the servants of the poor secretly pronounced the vows of religious life, intending to consecrate to the Lord not only their work but also themselves.

21. Sattin, p. 14. A notarized document, dated Dec. 24, 1737, proves that Mme Marie Badet, widow of Jacques Seguin, was living in the LeVerrier house. (Archives of the Grey Nuns of Montreal, no. 351).

Chapter VI

POOR AMONG THE POOR

Marguerite remained in relative anonymity because her life was so closely involved with the poor for whom she cared. But there are many details of the persecution her efforts encountered; and they fully justify the title of 'valiant woman' granted to her, the soul of the undertaking. Seven years would elapse, however, before Marguerite would let anyone know how she interpreted those events stemming from the malice of men and those other mysterious occurrences permitted by God Himself which put His servant's trust to the test.

A fire broke out in the LeVerrier house during the night of January 31, 1745. After warning the others, Mme d'Youville barely succeeded in saving herself, "shod in a slipper and an old shoe." In a short time, the house became an inferno, and the laywomen saw the flames destroy their home. A few moments before, it had been filled with ten boarders. [1] Now, for shelter they had the cold snow; for consolation, their own survival; and for encouragement, the sarcastic remarks of the curious who hurried to the scene and saw heaven's punishment in this tragedy. 'This will finally drive these wanton women from this house — adventurers who, under

---

1. In July, 1739, the household included ten poor women. (Dufrost, 1st manuscript, p. 10).

the mask of charity, give themselves over to trading in liquor.' This explains the name of 'soeurs grises' (tipsy nuns), given to them in derision. The renown of the daughters of St. Vincent de Paul — also known as "Soeurs Grises" — had already crossed the Atlantic; and, at one time, the colonists had hoped they would come. [2] "But why feel pity for these public sinners who get drunk, who pick quarrels, who give themselves over to all kinds of excesses?"

Furthermore, why not give full vent to the opposition against them, particularly since the petition of 1738? Then, the leading citizens of Montreal, among them Mme d'Youville's two brothers-in-law, unreservedly voiced their objections to the plan "of the priests of Montreal" — the substitution of the Grey Nuns for the Nursing Brothers at the General Hospital. [3] The Sulpicians were not spared, either. It was said that they were the ones who furnished the Sisters with brandy. And, rumor had it that during that terrible night you could see the alcohol burning in the violet flames shooting from the inferno.

These insinuations and insults could not shock Marguerite. She had heard still others since she had opened her doors to the poor women of Montreal. Slander worked so well that the Grey Nuns were refused Holy Communion at the Recollet's church. But it must have been especially painful to listen to these accusations when the aged poor and their

2. Mem. des Interessez (sic) à la pêche de l'Acadie, 1689. (Coll. des doc. relatifs à l'histoire de la N.-F., vol. 1, p. 393). Even more recently the name had been used to refer to the lay sisters who belonged to the Congrégation de Notre-Dame (Jamet, A., OSB, *Marguerite Bourgeoys*, p. 682).
3. Complete text of the petition is found in Angers, pp. 63-65.

servants were trembling with cold and wondering with good reason where they would spend the rest of that terrible night.

Certainly, during those days of 1737, they expected trials. That was why Mme d'Youville had recommended, in one of the first entries on the loose-leaf pages of the rule "to make the sign of the cross on oneself and on one's heart to imprint there the love of Jesus' cross." It became customary to recite the salutation to the sign of the redemption after Communion: O Cross, our only hope, all hail! And crosses they had.

One of the first members fell victim to the hard work and prolonged fasts; Catherine Cusson died on February 20, 1741. [4] The Foundress herself, victim of an undiagnosed knee infection, was obliged to reduce her activities at the beginning of 1738. Her sons, who were also ill, were taken into this refuge of the poor, one after the other. [5] M. Normant's life was in danger; his death would have compromised the very existence of their work. In this emergency, Mme d'Youville prayed to "her usual source of help, the Father of Mercies, promising to order a painting of Him from France" if the priest's recovery was granted. [6]

And joy followed the cross, as it always did in Marguerite's life. Two new members, Sisters Rainville and Lasserre-Laforme, replaced Sister Cusson.

---

4. An old report entitled Ancien Journal, contains this significant detail: "One day, two of the Sisters fainted at the refectory table". p. 313.

5. In her will, dated Oct. 8, 1757, Mme d'Youville thanked her companions for the limitless care they took of her children during the illnesses they endured when they were young and for the care they gave her for seven years.

6. Faillon, p. 43.

The knee infection which plagued her suddenly disappeared "without any human help" [7] at the end of 1744, just in time to allow her to escape the fire. M. Normant was restored to health, and the candle which burns November 21, every year since 1741, in the Church of Notre Dame, will always commemorate this.

As always, the Sisters found their joy especially in caring for the poor women. They praised the Lord for the fact that persecution and slander had not limited their opportunities to serve. They received frequent requests for their services. They supplied clothing for the French troops and for the explorers of the West. [8] Their sewing supported their patients. This role of "little representatives of Providence" consoled them from the hostility of the people of Montreal, some of whose relatives had found a refuge in the LeVerrier home. Among them, there was a retarded woman who was suddenly seized with the urge to look for her slippers. She returned to the burning house and there met a horrible death.

A trial coming from the misunderstanding of men may be understandable. How much faith is needed to accept an inexplicable misfortune brought on without any human cause. Faced with the destruction of her house and the irreparable tragedy of the loss of a human life, Marguerite might have asked herself whether she ought not put an end to her work. It seemed that God Himself was taking from her the means of going on. But, doubt never crossed her mind. She stood in the dark night, lit up only by the flames, and she comforted the poor old women,

7. Sattin, p. 18.

8. Morice: *L'Église catholique dans l'ouest Canadien*, vol. 1, pp. 294-295.

promising not to abandon them. The mocking words and sarcastic remarks heaped upon her, the widow of the former fur trader, did not arouse her. Always concerned for others, she expressed her fear that the fire might spread to the neighboring houses; and when everything had burned and the dying flames lit up only shadows, another light glowed in Marguerite's heart. She understood the message: "The disciple is not above the Master" (Mt. 10:24); and since it was her wish to follow Him, like Him she would "have nowhere to lay her head" (Lk. 9:58). This was the Gospel precept she quoted in the fourth article of the document describing the attitudes with which the Sisters were to conduct themselves.

Serving the poor means adopting their uncertain and insecure situation; it means not only offering one's help but also putting at their disposal everything one has: goods, talents, aptitudes, life itself. It means throwing in one's lot with theirs, not sporadically nor temporarily, but permanently. And Marguerite realized that she had not given everything. Humbly, she admitted: "We were too comfortable, perhaps even too attached to the things of the world; from now on we will live more in common, more poorly," she said to her companions. [9] Immediately, she decided to obey this sign from God to give up everything and "to commit herself forever to serve her masters, the poor". To them the Sisters would devote all their attention and care.

As though the Lord were only waiting for this resolution to strengthen his servant, a rich Montreal merchant, M. Fonblanche, offered her a house, rent-free, where she could continue her work. The cross, once again, was a herald of joy for the Grey Nuns

---

9. Sattin, p. 19.

who found themselves reunited under the same roof with those to whom they devoted their lives. Relatives and friends they still had who provided the necessary household articles and furniture while "the priests of Montreal" provided their meals.

Perhaps they may have been able to save some pieces of furniture from the fire. One thing is certain: the statue of Our Lady of Providence was not destroyed. Under Mary's patronage, Marguerite and her companions drew up at once the solemn promises we know as the Original Commitment (engagements primitifs). In it, they gave everything to the Lord's poor.

"We, the undersigned, for the greater glory of God, the salvation of our souls and the relief of the poor, sincerely desiring to leave the world and to renounce everything we own to consecrate ourselves unreservedly to the service of the poor, have joined together in the bonds of the purest charity, not wishing to form a new community, to live and die together (and) have unanimously agreed and promised, of our own free will, what follows".

And by "what follows" they committed themselves: "to live henceforth together for the remainder of our lives in perfect union and charity, under the guidance of those (superiors) who will be given to us; in the observance of our rule of life; in poverty and total detachment; putting in common everything we now possess and will possess in the future, not keeping the right of ownership or the right to dispose of it; by this document, making a pure, simple and irrevocable gift of it to the poor; to devote unreservedly our time, our days, our effort, our very life to work; whose income put in common, will provide for the support of the poor and of ourselves; to shelter, feed and support as many poor people as we are capable of helping." And they specified "that all who join us will bring with them what they own in order to put it to common use, renouncing all rights of ownership by the voluntary and irrevocable gift they will make of it to the members of Jesus Christ. Should it happen that a member might return to the world, for a good reason, she will be satisfied with what we will have the charity to give her." Finally, if in the future, this work should come to an end, it is understood that "possessions, furnishings and buildings belonging to this house are to be handed over to the Superior of the Seminary of Montreal to be used in good works and especially for the relief of the poor." [10]

In drafting this Original Commitment, Mme d'Youville asked M. Normant's help who wasted no time. They postponed the signing of the document to the feast of the Purification of Our Lady, that is, two days after the fire which destroyed everything except the faith, hope and love of these servants of the poor. Now, freed of useless attachments to things and to worldly security, they would henceforth give themselves entirely to the care of the Heavenly Father in fulfilling the work He had entrusted to them.

"Having read and re-read this document uniting us, we approve it and we commit ourselves with our whole heart to carry out its provisions with the Lord's grace." Thus concludes the document which Marguerite and Sisters Demers and Lasource [11] signed February 2, 1745.

10. The complete text of the Original Commitment is given in the appendix.
11. The latter signed under the name of Sr. Thaumur. The Commitment would be signed by every Grey Nun the day of her religious profession.

Under the inspiration of the Holy Spirit, Marguerite had just passed a milestone on her way to God. Unquestionably, she was the leader of the group, their inspiration, with everything the term implies. It was up to her to discern the signs which invited her and her companions to new growth in holiness. She fulfilled this call. And the Lord, Sovereign Master, seemed eager to put the sincerity of these commitments to the test.

Three times in less than two years, the Grey Nuns had to move from one house to another. They were always pursued by the ill-will of some groups in the city, until the day when they assumed the administration of the General Hospital. Did Marguerite wish to share the lot of the poor? She entered the hospital, dispossessed, lying on a poor mattress placed on a cart. Successive trials did not weaken her courage, but they did exhaust her strength and even threatened her life. Once again, it seemed, she was faced with the challenge of another paradox: undertaking the rebuilding of a house in ruins, as M. du Lescoät had told her earlier, at a time when she had all she could do to stay alive herself.

The Foundress was no longer surprised at situations which seemed apparently hopeless. Her experience of the previous ten years had brought her to wonder at "the incomprehensible resources of Providence," [12] which acts in hopeless cases and "brings about marvels." Several years before she had begun the custom of reciting daily the Litany of Divine Providence. In these invocations the Sisters praised God's tender care, "the consolation of the poor, the strength of the· weak, the mother of the

---

12. Letter to the abbé de l'Isle-Dieu, Oct. 17, 1768.

orphan and solace of our life." [13] To judge by the dog-eared pages of her personal copy she frequently recited the Office of Divine Providence; she did not however require the Sisters to recite it. But the theme recurs over and over again. "The Lord is my shepherd; nothing shall I want." [14]

These words of confidence, of total self-giving, were the subject of her meditation. They developed in her soul that attitude of whole-hearted trust which alone could account for her great hope of restoring a ruined institution. When that work was finished, thanks to Providence, how many more poor they would be able to accommodate there! And the Foundress rejoiced in anticipation that she would be able to shelter both brothers and sisters of the human family, in greater numbers than before.

---

13. This litany is found in a book entitled: *La Dévotion au Sacré-Coeur de Jésus*, by J. Croiset, S.J., published in 1737. We can conclude that the recitation of the litany dates from 1740 or 1741.

14. Ibid., p. 511.

Chapter VII

SUFFERING

Mme d'Youville's son, Charles, said that his mother "had a gentle disposition." He added that this gentleness did not mean softness, cowardice, the fear of displeasing others or concern for personal popularity. On the contrary, he was careful to point out that "on occasion she knew how to be severe without setting aside Christian meekness." [1]

Marguerite meditated daily on one of the mysteries of Christ's passion. [2] Like Him, she chose to answer the insults and shabby treatment directed against her with silence. But when her poor were attacked, she was not slow to assert their rights. The firmness, courtesy and humility which are evident in her correspondence from 1750 to 1752 let us realize to some degree the moral strength she must have had to remain silent when it would have been so easy for her to silence the voices of slander. She rather preferred "to cast all her cares into the bosom of God" [3] and to let her actions speak of her great respect for the unfortunate and the under-privileged. And rightly so. According to her own testimony, "the Lord seemed to accept the services of the Grey Nuns and favored them with the blessings he showered

---

1. Dufrost, 1st manuscript, p. 3.
2. Montgolfier, Constitutions, p. 107.
3. Invocations to Divine Providence.

on their labors and their care." [4] The shaky institution rose from its ruins and the prejudices of the Montreal opposition dissolved as the people saw the house "built by the devotion of their ancestors" come to life again.

Periods of calm were, however, brief in the life of this woman so well prepared for work and conflict. Soon, other obstacles appeared brought about by Bigot, a shrewd and clever character, who publicly announced his determination to destroy the General Hospital of Montreal. [5] Gossip brought to Ville-Marie the unacceptable ideas of the Intendant and, to defend themselves against so unjust a decision, the Grey Nuns drew up a petition. We might call Bigot's malevolence a "happy fault" for it left to posterity documents in which the Foundress explained the motives behind her actions and revealed at the same time the insight and understanding the Lord had given her. This would cause the abbé de l'Isle-Dieu to write later: "Mme d'Youville seems to be a person who grasps, understands and pursues the matter very well." [6]

So she wrote to their Excellencies, the Governor General and the Intendant of New France that: 1. the provisional agreement in 1747 had been accompanied

---

4. Petition of the Grey Nuns, undated. Some historians place it in 1751. An excerpt from the petition clearly indicates that it was drawn up before the ordinance of Oct. 15, 1750. This is Faillon's opinion, and he satisfies the requirements of historical research. Written in M. Normant's handwriting, it still expressed Mme d'Youville's ideas. To prove this, one need only compare this petition with the letter from the Superior of the Seminary to the officials on the same matter.

5. Letter of M. Normant to the Bishop of Québec, 1750. The details of these difficulties are restated in Faillon, pp. 70-86. Bigot was the Intendant of New France.

6. Quoted in Angers, p. 181.

by the formal promise to request its ratification at Court. 2. that the hospital, until then a general hospital only in name, had become one in fact since it housed not only the poor of both sexes but also the insane, incurables and even fallen women. 3. that the farms connected with the institution had been redeveloped. The progress made "thanks to the Lord's blessing" would continue, for she added: "The zeal of the Grey Nuns for the service of the poor whose servants they are proud to be has not diminished and now they are even more eager to devote their time, their work, and their lives to the support of this house."

The authorities planned to merge the General Hospital of Montreal with that of Quebec or another community. The Foundress expressed her admiration for the virtues and talents of the Sisters of Quebec. But she did not hesitate to protest against "the wrong done to the poor of the Montreal area who have a rightful claim to this house built for them," for the limited space in the Quebec hospital gave them little hope of being admitted. Such a solution would be contrary to the intentions of the founders and would certainly disappoint the faithful who had contributed to maintain this institution built "to take in the members of Jesus Christ."

The Foundress went still further and pointed out that such a decision could not be based on the need to economize, since it would be necessary to enlarge the hospital at Quebec. And finally she brought up the question of the debt of 38,000 pounds, contracted during the administration of the Nursing Brothers, and of the debts of approximately 10,000 pounds she was forced to contract in order to reconstruct the buildings. "If it is because you know of these debts that you fear that the institution may not be able to be maintained without the extra-ordinary help of the Court, the petitioners have the honor to tell you that they rely completely on Providence; they ask only your protection and the approval of His Majesty; they will gratefully receive the gifts and favors His Majesty may wish to grant them but they will not trouble anyone for money. Further, they will pay the debts within three years."

However, these difficulties prompted Mme d'Youville to be prudent. In return for these promises she asked that the Grey Nuns be permanently sub-stituted for the Brothers with the rights, graces and privileges mentioned in the letters patent; and she promised to give an annual account of the revenues and expenditures of the hospital as well as of the alms that would be given it.

These statements, with which the city and colonial governments would one day agree, did not change the decision of the officials at the time. Marguerite, whose "confidence was entirely in Providence" found that God was silent and that she had pleaded in vain. The order signed in Quebec, October 15, 1750, and published at Montreal, Nov-ember 23 of that year made the merger of the two hospitals official. What went on in her soul when she thought of the possibility of leaving the refuge where already so many unfortunate people had found shelter? Of course, there was always the possibility of resuming her activities as a social worker, for we know that in 1745 she had solemnly promised to consecrate her life to the service of the poor. [7]

The order stipulated that she would have to vacate the premises by July 1, 1751 and "make no repairs to the hospital under penalty of losing the

7. Article two of the Original Commitment.

cost of these." This last recommendation was late in coming, to say the least, for the repairs had already been completed and not without the knowledge of the authorities.

At the beginning of January, Mme d'Youville sent the financial statement of the hospital to the Intendant. Bigot refused to repay the funds spent to develop the farms. With unbelievable coolness, he reproached her for having taken in more than twelve poor people and complained to her of "having accepted women who, until then, had not been admitted there." He ordered her to sow the fields under the pretext that she had profited from the harvest herself when she first took office in 1747; and he ordered her to hire another farmer and to pay the pension due to Brother Joseph. [8]

Bigot, the clever strategist, defended himself by attacking. But if he thought the battle was won, he failed to understand the personality of this woman who had every intention of defending the truth. And the truth had been falsified, knowingly or unknowingly. Mother d'Youville gave the Intendant the benefit of the doubt, but she set forth the facts "without exceeding the limits of Gospel meekness." And this is what gives her answer its undeniable quality of nobility and strength. Point by point, she refuted his accusations.

"Recall, Sir, I beg of you," she wrote, "that you have always required me to keep everything in good condition and to repair what needed repairs. His Excellency, the Bishop and His Lordship, the

---

8. Letter of Feb. 5, 1751. This pension owed to the only surviving member of the Charon Brothers was paid, according to the agreement, as indicated in the letter of Mme d'Youville to Bigot, April 12, 1751.

Governor, gave me the same order...I do not have your orders in writing," she added shrewdly, "but your word is as good as a written order; I relied on it as I was supposed to do because of the respect I owe you and my knowledge of your uprightness. I acted in accordance with this, and it seems to me that I am justified and that you cannot, before God and men, refuse to have me reimbursed for the sums I have borrowed and which I owe."

She had submitted her accounts to him beginning with her first year of administration. Then expenditures exceeded income, as was to be expected, since everything had to be repaired. If she had exceeded her authority, this should have been obvious in the first report. "On the contrary, you urged me to continue because you understood the need for this. Therefore I did not just act on my own; it was with your knowledge, under your supervision, and with your approval." It was even by the Intendant's order that experts were named to draw up the list of necessary repairs of which "only a small portion" were completed. With irrefutable logic, she continued: "If I had allowed the houses and the farms to fall into ruins and had stopped cultivating the land, you would have blamed me. I did what I thought was for the best, without self-interest, but only for the good of the poor. If I do not have the satisfaction of having satisfied you, it is not through ill-will but for lack of ability," she humbly admitted.

The number of the poor to be admitted had been fixed at twelve. The Foundress admitted that she had not been informed of this and emphasized that she had been granted the authorization to open a women's ward and to accommodate there those for whom she was already responsible. Furthermore, the Intendant could not plead ignorance on this subject.

During his stay in Montreal in 1749 he had visited the hospital, he had then seemed satisfied, and his words of encouragement had been interpreted as approval. Moreover, she added, the increase in the number of the poor had nothing to do with this matter, for "the inmates received what they needed, not from the fruit of the land, but by the care of Providence and our work," the Foundress declared.

As for her obligation to sow the fields, she pointed out that, contrary to Bigot's statement, she had not found them sown when she assumed her post as administrator. She considered herself obliged to leave things as she had found them. Moreover, the present tenant farmer was leaving, and she no longer had the necessary authority to hire a replacement. [9]

In the inscrutable ways of Providence this statement had no effect. In fact, things became more complicated for this mother of the poor. Bishop de Pontbriand, to whom she appealed, maintained a disconcerting neutrality in his letter of February 4, 1751. Some weeks later, he informed her that he did "not wish to get involved in this matter" after suggesting to her a serious suspicion: "I think that people are convinced that you have not really borrowed the money and that these expenditures were made with the alms which were given you." [10]

---

9. Rough copy, signed by Mme d'Youville herself and dated Feb. 16, 1751.

10. Letter of March 16, 1751. At first, the Bishop was in favor of Mme d'Youville. In a letter dated Sept. 8, 1748, he told her "that no better way can be found to revive the hospital than to leave it in her hands". He confided to the abbé de l'Isle-Dieu of Mme d'Youville: "She is one of those women of unusual worth and I think that the hospital will be well off in her hands". (Letter of the abbé to the Secretary of State, Feb. 22,

The blow struck home and obliged the Foundress to break with her usual reticence. From her own lips we learn what was in her character and what was not. These are her words:

"I am sincere, upright, incapable of any deception or restriction which could disguise the truth or give it a double meaning. Your Excellency, I have indeed borrowed 9,550 pounds for the maintenance and redevelopment of the lands of this hospital. I owe this money and there is no source of payment except the repayment which I expect from Your Excellency, and from these gentlemen. What I have the honor to tell you, Your Excellency, is the truth, and I would not tell the least lie for all the goods in the world. In this matter, I sought only to rebuild this hospital and its property. When I spent this money, I never intended to create a kind of necessity of keeping myself here, as some people think and are saying because it seems impossible to reimburse me. That is not my character, Your Excellency. I can assure you that I have never thought of it. Having been made responsible for this work, I should fear to answer for it before God if I allowed things to deteriorate." [11]

1749). His change in attitude was brought about by the opposition of the Court to the foundation of new religious communities, the belief that after Mme d'Youville's death, the group of lay women would disperse (Faillon, pp. 71 & 75) and the evil influence of Bigot. On his behalf, however, it should be stated that once truth won out, he did not hesitate to acknowledge the goodness of the Foundress and "to support her requests at Court". (La Jonquière to the Minister of the Navy, Oct. 19, 1751).

11. Signed rough draft of a letter addressed to the Bishop of Quebec, April 12, 1751. The passages omitted are concerned with the loan and are reproduced word for word in her letter to Bigot.

The day on which she wrote these lines, Marguerite handed over the buildings and lands of the farms at Pointe-St-Charles and Chambly to the acting administrator of the General Hospital of Quebec. She herself so informed Bigot, reiterating to him her explanations concerning the debt. It is easy to discern in this letter, the last she wrote concerning this matter, that she now knew what to expect from the trickery and the greed of the Intendant. At Ville-Marie, people did not scruple to blame the official openly but that did not alter in the least the Foundress' courtesy towards him.

He alleged that he had not examined the accounts because she had not asked him to do so. "The fact that I sent them to you was of itself a request", the Foundress noted; and she added: "I believe, however, that I expressed this request in the letter which accompanied the accounts." The property of the General Hospital was non-transferable, Bigot agreed; however, he authorized the sale of the house, the courtyard and the gardens. "I have difficulty in reconciling the two opinions," observed the Foundress shrewdly. [12] Henceforth, she would let events follow their course. Bigot persisted in his first opinion; [13] no one was ignorant of this, just as everyone knew that he enjoyed almost absolute power in the colony. To continue this correspondence would have been useless and it was not in Marguerite's character to prolong her regrets. This would be evident later in life, when, concerning a difficult trial she would say to her correspondents: "this is a thing of the past; let us speak of it no longer." [14]

---

12. Signed rough draft of a letter addressed to Bigot, April 12, 1751.
13. La Jonquière to the Minister, Oct. 19, 1751.
14. Letters of Aug. 28, Nov. 5, 1765, and of August, 1766.

She had no illusions about the seriousness of the matter; it was a question of the destruction or survival of her work. But, in her mind, the problem went beyond its human dimensions. It was for God to indicate His will. For her part, "she kept her soul in silence and peace before him," (Ps. 131:2) according to the habit she had acquired long ago. In this decision a significant aspect of Marguerite's spirituality is clear. Her soul filled with faith and hope, she knew with absolute certainty that her destiny, like that of her poor, was in the hands of that "all loving Father" [15] who would "preserve this house, the refuge of the unfortunate." [16]

And that is why, in the midst of this suffering, despite the uneasiness and the anguish which assailed her, Marguerite clung to an unchanging God in the depths of her soul. It is not surprising that people admired "the profound calmness of her soul which the serenity of her face reflected" and they attributed "this wonderful tranquility to her unquestioning confidence in Providence." [17]

---

15. Pope John XXIII, Apostolic Letter; p. 3.
16. Letter to Mr. C. Héry, June 15, 1765.
17. Dufrost, 1st manuscript, p. 20.

Chapter VIII

VICTORY

Marguerite saw the difficulties threatening her work disappear as if by magic. But she did not express her joy, at least in writing. As we read her correspondence, we find that she was not one of those people who take gifts for granted; her letters are full of expressions of gratitude. The only letter she wrote during these decisive years was addressed to the colonial authorities. To express her joy would have seemed to gloat over her victory, and that was hardly consistent with her attitude. What she wanted was to "maintain an establishment so useful to Montreal... to welcome the sick, the aged of both sexes" [1] as she stated so simply in her memorandum to the authorities! With the same simplicity, she confided to them that "Providence, our work, the good will of many people willing to help this house" constituted the resources they counted on to assure the smooth running of the hospital. [2] Her restraint and modesty in this unusual situation are admirable; she had won a total victory. The Court had both admitted the truth of what she claimed and also authorized the foundation of a new religious community. The Foundress indicated, however, that this involved rather the

---

1. Memorandum dated June 19, 1752.
2. Mme d'Youville communicated to the officials her plans for liquidating the institution's debts.

substitution of the Grey Nuns for the nursing brothers. [3] In short, what had been intended to destroy the work of Mme d'Youville and her companions became the point of departure toward official recognition and canonical approbation.

Marguerite realized that the Lord's goodness not only fulfilled her hopes but even exceeded them. Twice she had openly declared that she "did not wish to form a new community" [4] as she specified that these lay women would try to live as real religious "according to the interior dispositions of the heart." [5] Knowing how to distinguish the essential from the ephemeral, Marguerite fixed her desire on God and the things of God and walked under the guidance of the Holy Spirit in the way of the evangelical counsels toward the gift of self in a consecrated life. She was ready to take on the responsibilities of a Foundress, for she had followed the will of Providence day by day and the Lord had prepared her for them. Faced with this new evidence of divine foresight, Marguerite probably confided to her close friends what she would later write to the abbé de l'Isle-Dieu: "Providence is wonderful; it has incomprehensible motives; it provides for everything. In it is all my trust." [6]

It is especially regrettable that Mme d'Youville did not sketch the portrait of the ideal Grey Nun in a few concise sentences. To point up her typical characteristics, we must look to the testimony of her contemporaries, keeping in mind a memorandum in

---

3. Letters patent, art. 1, June 3, 1753.
4. Attitudes with which the Sisters should act, art. 2 and Original Commitment, 1st paragraph.
5. Attitudes, art. 13.
6. Letter of Oct. 17, 1768.

her own handwriting which she fortunately failed to destroy.

The heads of the hospital administration drew up several questions about articles to be included in the letters patent. Mme d'Youville wished to consult M. Normant, in accordance with the parenthetical clause in article two requesting the Superior of the Seminary "to be good enough to be always the (Superior) of the Grey Nuns." [7] Her annotations indicate that justice, equity, human feeling, psychological balance, religious consecration are more than mere words to her.

"What policy shall we follow with respect to lay women who remain free to withdraw" from the community or of "other persons whom we shall have to dismiss"? [8] "All have the right to what they brought with them," Mme d'Youville specified. "And if that is not enough to provide for themselves, we will compensate them according to the services they rendered." The Superior of the Seminary and the Superior of the Grey Nuns would submit any reasons for dismissal to the Bishop who would be responsible for making a final decision.

It is clearly understood that "no person for reason of illness" can ever be dismissed any more than one could send away "the courageous and willing invalids", for experience had proved that "they do as much work as the others."

Before the number of members to be admitted could be determined, they would have to know what works the Court would allow the Sisters to undertake.

---

7. Signed Memorandum, undated but probably drawn up in 1752, shortly after the ordinance of 1750 was rescinded.
8. Letters patent, art. 11.

The care of the aged of both sexes, of girls and women who were prostitutes, visiting the sick at home and in the hospital especially during epidemics — this was not enough for the Foundress. [9] She planned to take care of "foundlings, epileptics, lepers, those afflicted with ulcers and others."

This enumeration proves that now there were no limits to Marguerite's love. She wanted to help all her brothers and sisters, no matter what trial afflicted them. Until then, because of the limitations of space and of other resources, she had been forced to concern herself only with the most urgent cases. But she carefully avoided thinking that she was destined to serve only one category of unfortunate persons. In the initial rule of life and in the Original Commitment which faithfully reflect her ideas, she insisted on the total availability of the Grey Nun for the poor. And it is clear that for her, anyone who suffers in body or spirit is poor. Seen in the light of faith, the unfortunate individual took on a divine dimension in her eyes; he was a "member of Jesus Christ" and the Grey Nun "should be proud to be his servant." [10] On this subject, her ideas developed as her charism, her specific vocation became clearer. She set down what she understood by religious consecration in the eighth article of this memorandum. Asked to speak to the question of the members' possessions, she wrote: "Since we are spouses of the poor who are members of Jesus Christ, our Spouse,

---

9. The hospital took in the insane, and, according to the Memorandum of M. Montgolfier to Thomas Gage of Oct. 28, 1760, one ward was set aside for victims of venereal diseases.

10. Her petition of 1750.

all our goods should be held in common." [11]
Religious consecration, mystical marriage, total gift
of self to God through these "little ones" (Mt. 25:40)
who are "Christ's brothers" — that is the vocation
of the Grey Nun who is called to work in the Church,
as Marguerite herself described it. Though brief,
this formula is complete. It synthesizes the teaching
she gave those who were attracted by her ideal and
came to learn from her. Seeing her life, treasuring
her words, her companions learned from her "to
know God the Father by recognizing the Son"
(1 Jn. 2:23). For the "extraordinary interior attraction
of grace" with which she had been gifted in 1727
"continued to grow". At this crucial point when she
defined the characteristic spirit of her community,
she invited her Sisters "to learn from the heart of the
Father the attitudes of love, tender concern and compassion they should have for the poor, the sick, and
the orphans." To reach "the universal Source of every
perfect gift," [12] the Grey Nun was to choose the
only way — Christ Himself. The Foundress wished to
conform herself to Christ. So, under the guidance
of the Holy Spirit, she committed herself to be the
humble instrument of His mercy. Like the Master
who came "not to be served but to serve", Marguerite
meant to express her love by a life of total, selfless
devotion, of service to God's children who were
members of the great human family. [13] Now she
no longer "walked in the darkness" as at the begin-

---

11. Mme d'Youville did not win her case, for art. 11 of the letters
     patent stipulates that the lay women would keep ownership
     of their patrimony.

12. Faillon, p. 19 and p. 268.

13. Here we must note the influence of *Le petit livre de vie* by
     P. A. Bonnefons, s.j. on Marguerite during the important
     years of 1750 to 1755. The passages from the Gospels and the

ning of her apostolate. She could say that she had "found her place in the Church", like Thérèse of Lisieux. She, too, would be love, drawn from the heart of God, made tangible by the care she lavished on the poor. To show the Sisters that this was really the reason for their life, the Foundress wanted to have the heart of Christ, symbol of love, placed above the corpus on their silver profession cross. [14] For some time, devotion to the Cross and to the Sacred Heart had been practiced in the General Hospital. The Nursing Brothers of the Cross and of St. Joseph celebrated the feasts of the Finding and of the Exaltation of the Cross as their congregational feasts. In the church, a chapel had been dedicated to the Sacred Heart. [15] Marguerite recognized that here she had found the basic elements of her own spirituality. She probably concluded that the work of rebuilding to which God destined her was not

---

excerpts from the Imitation of Christ quoted by the author almost all deal with the glory of service. It is significant that Mme d'Youville ordered a copy of the book from France for her usual confidante, Sister Lasource. The latter stated from whom she received it: "from my beloved Mother who gave it as only she can give."

14. Faillon, p. 272.

15. A copy of an inventory of 1719, lists this chapel without indicating the date of its blessing. It may date back to the period when Joseph de la Colombière, brother of Blessed Claude de la Colombière who was the director of Saint Margaret Mary Alacoque, stayed there. He became the spiritual director of the Charon Brothers in 1698 and in his will stipulated that, should he die in Montreal, his heart was to be buried in this chapel. He died in Quebec in 1723. (Cf. Fauteux, Sr. A., L'hôpital général de Montréal, vol. 1, pp. 36-38). As for the feasts of the cross, Faillon claims that only the Finding of the Cross was celebrated. Mme d'Youville herself must have added the celebration of the Exaltation and obtained a plenary indulgence for these two feasts, August 11, 1767.

merely material but especially spiritual. It was to be carried out in the spirit of the Hospital's founders.

The Nursing Brothers had led lives filled with work. This explains their devotion to Joseph, the humble carpenter of Nazareth. The Confraternity of the Holy Family held this devotion in special honor, and Marguerite developed it in harmony with her special grace. She saw St. Joseph as the earthly father, a human presence like that of the Eternal Father for Jesus and Mary, the providence who sustained them. This man of silence was a contemplative blessed by the visible presence of the Son of God and of his mother. His humble work contributed to the growth of the world's Savior. One day the Foundress would express these ideas clearly and creatively. She wanted to have a picture painted depicting St. Joseph at his work bench with his tools while a cross appeared above the figure of the child Jesus. [16]

Her other choices pointed out still more clearly how important humility was to her. She chose the title "Grey Nuns" rather than "Ladies of Charity" as suggested by Bishop de Pontbriand. She wanted the dress to be grey to remind the Sisters who would wear it of the modest beginnings of the little society. The headpiece, made of a piece of white material and "a kind of bonnet of black gauze" was an innovation. The Foundress did not wish to adopt the traditional veil. "Since the Grey Nun is expected to render

---

16. Letter to M. Maury, Sept. 21, 1771. It seems that the Foundress preferred visualizations to long explanations. The painting of the Eternal Father, the profession cross and this plan for a painting of St. Joseph indicate that for her "a picture is worth a thousand words".

all kinds of services at any time to the poor, to go through the streets and to work in the kitchen and in other manual work, it was, in her opinion, more appropriate to wear simply a bonnet." [17]

The Bishop of Quebec approved their dress during his visit, June 15, 1755, and signed the Rule, the Original Commitment and the Dispositions with which the Sisters were to conduct themselves. [18] He expressed his satisfaction at the improvements made to the hospital, the eagerness of each Sister and especially their gentleness toward prostitutes. [19]

Two years earlier Bishop de Pontbriand had written to Mme d'Youville: "You are too fair-minded to have any doubts about the sentiments of affection and respect I am proud to have for you." [20] Doubtless he wished to erase the memory of difficult times and allowed the Sisters to put on the habit immediately. But as an expression of gratitude for M. Normant, the Foundress postponed the clothing ceremony to August 25, the Superior's name day. Here again, she showed the delicacy of her feeling for the priest she would one day call "our Founder". [21] Then, the Sisters put on the grey dress, adjusted the crucifix which bore at each extremity the fleur-de-lis in honor of Louis XV who granted the letters patent. They slipped on their finger the silver ring, "symbol of the new and sacred bond which the Eternal Father himself created by uniting them

---

17. Faillon, p. 110.
18. Documents referred to as loose-leaf sheets.
19. Mandate issued June 15, 1755. In Jan. 1749, Mme Bégon mentioned the conversion of four women from "Jericho", the hospice for prostitutes.
20. Letter of Jan. 1753.
21. Letter to Sir Guy Carleton, Sept. 23, 1771.

to His Son as spouses for time and for eternity." [22]

The Grey Nuns expressed their joy by living out the gift of self they had just reaffirmed — by risking their lives. An epidemic of small-pox had just broken out. They opened their doors to the sick and went to nurse them in their homes. [23] One of them, Sr. Agathe Véronneau, contracted the disease which was complicated by typhus. This affected her mind and finally brought about her death. [24] Since the first days of their work, two Sisters had given to the poor "the greatest proof of love." If the emptiness caused by their loss pained these women united by the "bond of the most pure charity," they were not surprised. The Lord accepted the offering they had made of "their time, their work, their talents, their very life," [25] in serving the unfortunate.

22. Faillon, p. 271.
23. Angers, p. 141.
24. Archives of the Grey Nuns, file of Sr. A. Véronneau.
25. Original Commitment, 1st paragraph.

Chapter IX

LOVE WITHOUT LIMITS

In the introduction to his first manuscript, Charles Dufrost emphasized "the universal charity of Mme d'Youville." It "led her," he said, "to seek eagerly and seize joyfully every opportunity to help her neighbor." He noted further "the uncommon diligence which made her find resources for her poor even in situations which seemed hopeless." In his two memoranda, he declared "that Providence inspired in her a love of unremitting work which obliged her to take time from her sleep to help the suffering members of the Savior." [1]

"My Father works always and I also work" (Jn. 5:17) said the Master. Marguerite found inspiration in His example and did not recoil from any kind of work provided that it was honest. For some years the word had spread: "Go to the Grey Nuns; they refuse nothing." Consulting the record of admissions, one might also add that they refused no one. The Foundress took it on herself to adapt her services to the needs that presented themselves. The blind, the mute, the crippled, the chronically ill, the feeble-minded, negroes, epileptics, orphans, foundlings, slaves, Pawnees, Iroquois, and (even before the French and English war) Englishmen and Irishmen

---

1. Dufrost, 1st manuscript, pp. 9-10 and 2nd manuscript, p. 9.

were admitted to the hospital. [2] There are historical records of 'special cases', like the man called Héroux whose relatives Marguerite housed so that he could work and another, Picard, endowed with an immense appetite whom she hired as a carpenter. [3]

The universality of her charity and the number and variety of her works could not be separated; one came from the other. For her, works of charity perfectly expressed the quality and intensity of her love. God's movement in her heart rooted there once and for all the desire to devote herself to the well-being of others. On this she spoke clearly the day she promised to "devote unreservedly her time, her days, her efforts, her very life, to work" [4] in order to provide for the support of the poor. For, in her mind, the poor man was Christ; [5] and she intended to serve him with all the resourcefulness of her gifts and the generosity of her being.

God had especially gifted Marguerite for a life of activity and so He chose to make use of this natural disposition. Some passages in her letters indicate this fact. She assures the authorities of the future stability of the hospital, mentioning as guarantees "the care of Providence and our work." [6] "A good boy who knows how to work," she would say of one of her acquaintances. [7] And it is easy to sense her satisfac-

---

2. For example, Elizabeth, an Englishwoman, admitted in 1747 and Denis McCarthy, admitted in 1750.

3. Anc. Journal, v. 1, pp. 54-55.

4. Original Commitment, art. 2.

5. "Since we are spouses of the poor who are members of Jesus Christ, our Spouse". (Memorandum of 1752).

6. To Bigot, Feb. 16, 1751 and to the administrators, June 19, 1752.

7. Letter to Dr. A.-F. Feltz, Sept. 22, 1770. She is referring to M. Augustin Chaboyer.

tion as she praised Mme Robineau de Portneuf "who is more than eighty-one years old, who fasts and abstains on the days required and who works as we do for the good of the poor even though she pays her board."[8] These few lines reveal that Marguerite particularly valued "the holy work of one's hands" as a book in the Nursing Brothers' library called it. She was so convinced of the ascetical value of work that she did not feel it was necessary to set down any other kinds of penance for her religious family.

Is there a better way for a Grey Nun to reach that "total detachment" required for her service than by work? It is as imperative as a call to battle; even as it fills the day, it supports the works of charity. Work detaches the person, frees us and channels our energies. It makes light of personal preferences, of fatigue, even of exhaustion. On one condition, however — that it is not a showy activism or the feverish activity of a busy-body, dangers the Foundress knew well. So she insisted in the first article of the rule on the need for personal union with the Lord, for an interior dialogue between God and each Sister. This dialogue was to continue while she worked. During this time of prayer, the Sister opens herself to God's merciful love to pour it out on the needy persons she sees around her without judging them. [9] She can give only what she herself receives,

---

8. Letter to the abbé de l'Isle-Dieu, July 1769. Mme de Portneuf, that is Marguerite-Philippe de Muy, was Mme d'Youville's mother's first cousin. It is rather amusing to note that, speaking of the English, the Superior expressed the following opinion: "These people do not provide work, and their King even less". Letter to M. Débarras, Sept. 16, 1764.

9. "She had a truly charitable and compassionate attitude, not a purely natural compassion but one that she always referred to God", Charles Dufrost declared on p. 3 of his 1st manuscript.

but she gives it joyfully and generously. So we should not be surprised that Mme d'Youville attached such great importance to the spirit of work in the candidates who wanted to join her. "We will not send away invalids who are courageous and willing," she wrote in 1752, "since they do as much (work) as the others."

To the enterprises already in existence at the hospital, Mme d'Youville added many other undertakings. [10] Some called her a business woman when they saw her creativity. But those close to her knew better. They saw in her a "woman possessed by God who goes straight ahead, straining with all her being" to take possession of Him (Ph. 3:13).

She did not need to give commands, for she led others less by her words than by her example. "Nor did she hesitate to share with her Sisters the most menial work." [11] At all hours of the day she was a servant in every sense of the word. Bigot would have the opportunity to find this out, in an incident which shows that the Foundress had a sense of humor. The official came to order her to admit enemy as well as French soldiers. He did not announce his visit. The Foundress went to the parlor in her work clothes; she was busy "dipping candles." With an amused smile she answered the Sister who suggested that she change her clothing: "I did not know in advance that the Intendant was coming. He will forgive me and will have to see me just as I am. None of this will keep him from speaking with me." [12] She must have

10. The Hospital took in women boarders, and the Sisters, besides their sewing, made vestments, hosts, candles, artificial flowers and wax images of the Child Jesus. The farm lands were rented out for pasture and they also sold building materials.

11. Faillon, p. 284.

12. Sattin, pp. 35-36. The incident occurred in 1756.

been delighted with this stroke of luck — an opportunity to do an act of humility and to prove to the official that he could really count on "our work."

Under Marguerite's roof, the poor man was king. Everything was intended for him for he was the master who held first place. Did she not state in article two of the Original Commitment "that the income from the Sisters' work will be put in common to provide for the support of the poor and of... ourselves"? When foodstuffs grew scarce because of the war, the Sisters were satisfied with corn — to keep the wheat bread for the poor. [13] The Foundress would one day express the regret that she "did not have enough bed-sheets for the poor and for... ourselves." [14] When she realized that someone had installed a shelf to hold the cup from which the Sisters drank, she asked that it be removed. During her visits, she usually drank from the same cup as the poor and knew there was no shelf for their cup. "It is not right for the Sisters to be better off than they are." [15]

Such was her kindness, her compassion, that "they tried to keep her with them by holding on to her apron." And when "a person of social position and a poor person asked for her in the parlor at the same time, she did not hesitate and first went to the poor person." [16]

Respectful of the dignity of each individual, she let the patients who wanted to, share in the work of the house, according to their physical strength. She

---

13. Faillon, pp. 150-151.
14. Letter to M. C. Héry, Sept. 24, 1770.
15. Sattin, p. 48.
16. Faillon, pp. 290-291.

sensed how difficult it is for some people to be unable to pay for their keep. Tactfully and justly, she paid her volunteer workers a fair amount for their services. [17]

To the companions — her collaborators — Mme d'Youville showed "tender affection and much friendship." [18] They were souls chosen by God and indispensable co-workers in their common effort. Servants, the "hired help", were really part of this select team and they realized this from the Foundress' courtesy toward them and from the sensitivity which led her to offer them small gifts each New Year's Day. [19] Sensing in some of these helpers unusual aptitude for serving the poor, she asked Bishop de Pontbriand for permission to admit them as though into the community but without increasing the number of full members which had been limited to twelve. This would mean creating a subordinate membership; and the reasons she enumerated in favor of this innovation point to a keen psychological insight. Authorizing them to wear the Sisters' dress, she felt, would assure them of a certain respect from the patients; this would lead them to behave with greater seriousness and in a manner worthy of the nursing profession. This symbol of their belonging to the religious personnel of the house would encourage them to keep its interests at heart and would create in these young women a kind of spirit of emulation. They would then ask to be received into the community. To distinguish them from the Sisters (for the Foundress knew that the Court did not intend to increase the number of Sisters), they would not be given the profession cross.

---

17. These amounts are listed in the financial records.
18. Sattin, p. 48.
19. Financial records, gifts in addition to regular wages.

The Bishop recognized the wisdom of these suggestions and granted more than she asked. He suggested the formation of three or four orders within the community. [20] Some months later, he responded affirmatively to the Superior's request for permission to enlarge the hospital. These words of praise accompanied his answer: "I admire, Madame, your trust in Providence. I have remarked evidences of it since I have had the honor of knowing you." [21]

In this house devoted to Providence, a real spirit of unity reigned and this brought about wonders. For even after war was declared, they managed to provide three meals a day for this large family. Only God knows the cost to the Sisters, for they suffered in silence. But events do let us pierce this secrecy. In the fall of 1757 Marguerite's health deteriorated from over-work. Her condition was so serious that she dictated a will in which one of her remarkable personality traits stands out. She left her possessions to her companions to compensate them "for the numerous attentions they showed to her children whom they took care of when they were young, and for the care they took of her during the seven years she was obliged to remain in her room because of her knee infection." [22]

It is said that a noble soul can be known by its capacity for gratitude. Marguerite was not a person who easily forgot a kindness. Twenty years had

---

20. This idea was not carried out, at least immediately. The automatic replacement of the administrators by these aides involved a certain risk, since all were not suited to running the hospital. The Bishop's answer was dated May 24, 1758.

21. Letter of Jan. 7, 1758.

22. Will dated Oct. 8, 1757; reproduced in Angers, pp. 334-335.

passed since the events she recalled. But she did recall them and was anxious to stress them. Moreover, by naming the companions the Lord had given her as her sole heirs, she could be sure that everything would be used for the greater good of the poor.

The Foundress survived this illness to confront a very dramatic situation. Without realizing it, she exhibited a universal charity which devotes itself to all who suffer without distinction of race, creed or color. She lavished her care on the invaders whom the members of her family were courageously fighting. She offered shelter to Redcoats pursued by the Indians. She saved "John, the Englishman," from the stake; without her, he would have undergone unspeakable tortures. Likewise, Mme O'Flaherty and her two year old daughter, Marie-Louise, were freed through the efforts of M. de Lavalinière, the Sulpician, [23] and were received at the hospital. Southworth found an unexpected haven under the tent intended for the French army which the Grey Nuns were sewing together in their community room. [24]

While the enemy vise tightened around the capital, Quebec, and the food supply proved inadequate, the Foundress found a way of saving the English prisoners. Six of them were employed at the hospital, one as a mason and the others as orderlies. Twenty-one worked the farm at St. Charles and another, the farm at Chambly. [25] Tirelessly she continued her work of love, despite the devastating

23. Faillon, p. 145. Mme d'Youville had to pay two hundred pounds to ransom John from his captors. Marie-Louise became a Grey Nun, Dec. 19, 1776.

24. Ibid., p. 147.

25. Ibid., p. 146.

news which arrived at the end of the summer of 1759. Her son, Charles Dufrost, the priest, had been taken prisoner and was on an English vessel; [26] and her cousin, René Robineau de Portneuf, also a priest and pastor of the parish of St. Joachim, was killed August 23 "while leading his parishioners in an attempt to defend the village against the sorties and hostilities the enemy perpetrated there." [27]

Some weeks later the cry went up: "The country has fallen!" [28] It marked the disappearance of the common people's last hope; for, until then, they had thought that France was invincible.

The Foundress had known many trials during her lifetime. But what were they in comparison with this national tragedy which plunged her once again into total insecurity? Years later, disclosures would escape her which let us guess at the anguish which racked her soul in these tragic moments. "We were shocked; we had always deluded ourselves that France would not abandon us. We were deceived in our expectations." [29] And in another letter: "I would find comfort (in such great misfortune) if we returned to France." [30]

But a revealing action would indicate where she based her faith, where her hope stood firm, where

---

26. Trudel, M.: *L'Église canadienne sous le régime militaire*, v. 1, pp. 55-56.

27. Ibid., pp. 61-62. René Robineau de Portneuf was the son of Mme de Portneuf of whom Mme d'Youville spoke so highly.

28. Written by Sr. Ste-Hélène, OSU, (M. Charlotte de Muy), sister of Mme Robineau de Portneuf and, so, a relative of Mme d'Youville.

29. Letter to M. Villars, Aug. 5, 1763. The signing of the treaty ceding Canada to England had just been found out, although it was signed in Feb. 1763.

30. To Dr. A.-F. Feltz, Sept. 24, 1770.

she sought love. Filled with sorrow, she added two chapels to the transepts of the church — one dedicated to the Father of Mercies and one to the Sacred Heart. [31]

Because she was sure that God is really a Father, Marguerite continued to believe in human brotherhood despite war, mourning and separation.

---

31. Financial records, expenditures of the period 1760-1761.

Chapter X

DAUGHTER OF THE CHURCH

"Great is the suffering in the kingdom of France," Péguy's Joan said of her country. This statement applied to France's North American colony during the dismal years of 1759 and 1760. Everything was in jeopardy; the honor of an army which had fought courageously and the life of a people threatened with starvation. The capitulation of Quebec and the surrender of Montreal [1] ended the hostilities but did not ward off the specter of starvation. At the General Hospital, the work of the English prisoners who cultivated the farms postponed the period of famine. But this postponement was a short one for the "hired hands" recovered their freedom at the end of the war. The conqueror showed himself generous toward the religious communities of women to whom "he guaranteed the possession of their property" as well as "their constitutions and their privileges." [2] Nevertheless, to enjoy these, they still had to find a way to survive.

"Providence and our efforts are the resources we count on to support our work", Marguerite had said. [3] Now only Providence remained. With the

---

1. Quebec surrendered Sept. 13, 1759 and Montreal, Sept. 8, 1760.
2. Trudel, M., op. cit., v. 2 p. 416.
3. Memorandum of June 19, 1752.

repatriation of the French army, the hospital saw its principal source of income disappear. The time had come for Marguerite to prove that Providence was enough for her. Lacking written texts expressing her thoughts in the years from 1759 to 1761, we must interpret her acts and her deeds, and support this interpretation with letters written several years later.

Conscious that she was a woman of the Church, Marguerite relegated her personal misfortunes to the background in order to concern herself with the Church in the defeated colony. This was a Church without a shepherd since the death of Bishop de Pontbriand on June 8, 1760. The Bishop had left the capital, Quebec, during the autumn of 1759 and is believed to have stayed first at the General Hospital of Montreal and then at the Sulpician Seminary. [4] Nine priests, among them M. Louis Normant, died in 1759 [5] and twelve died the following year. So, in this period of two years, the number of priests declined from 196 to 163. [6] The silence of the British regarding men's communities darkened the picture. Nor could newly-ordained priests be counted on to fill the ranks of the clergy, for everything seemed to indicate that the naming of a Bishop would meet with serious obstacles. Added to this was a wave of

---

4. There may be a confirmation of this stay in the General Hospital in the Bishop's will which left to the Grey Nuns "all his church vestments: cinctures, ceremonial gloves, mitres, for they had made them, in whole or in part". (Will dated April 15, 1760).

5. Mme d'Youville was anxious to have a solemn funeral mass celebrated for the repose of the soul of the priest whom she called "the father and founder of this hospital". (Letter to M. A. Maury, Sept. 21, 1771).

6. Trudel, M., op. cit., v. 1. pp. 335 and 342.

licentiousness "which was at its peak" [7] as the number of illegitimate births indicated.

For these new needs, Marguerite found new solutions. Sick and aged priests and those reduced to poverty were welcomed to the hospital [8] and she assumed partial responsibility for the expenses of Pierre Mennard, a seminarian who went to France to continue his studies. [9]

Since 1752 she had been aware of the plight of the foundlings. She had then set forth in a report the reasons for undertaking this work. "We will take care of foundlings whose condition here is so unfortunate that of twenty who are baptized, only two or three survive. One can see that at the age of eighteen they are still ignorant of the basic truths of religion. I know some who are twenty-three years old who have not made their First Communion." It has been said that our zeal is in proportion to our love. In these few sentences, Marguerite gave the measure of hers. She knew that the Father welcomed these tiny children rejected by the world: the Son had redeemed them and, like her, they were called to share the Spirit of adoption. How could she not open her heart to them; how could she accept the possibility that they would never know the truths of faith which had

---

7. The Sisters of the Hôtel-Dieu to their Sisters at La Flèche, quoted by Faillon, p. 185.
8. The names of eight priests admitted from 1760 to 1771 are found in the records.
9. Angers, op. cit. p. 356, note 43. After this ordination April 7, 1764, the priest returned to Canada, June 6, 1764 and was successively parish priest at St. Jean, Ile d'Orléans, and at Chambly where he died June 28, 1792. He was the first in a series of young men intending to enter the priesthood and helped by the Grey Nuns who still continue to do this today.

been her source of strength ever since "it had pleased God" to reveal to her how really He is a Father?

Under the French regime, the authorities did not follow the suggestions of the proposal she submitted in 1752. This did not prevent the Foundress from caring for seventeen abandoned children from 1754 to 1759. But in the year 1760 alone, seventeen illegitimate births were registered, not including some terrible discoveries: children who had been drowned, stabbed to death or half-buried. [10] Everything pointed to a fresh outbreak of these atrocities and this spurred Mme d'Youville on to a new effort, this time directed at the English authorities. A report submitted to General Gage received his approval October 28, 1760, less than two months after the capitulation of Montreal. In this report drawn up by M. Montgolfier, the reasons set down by the Foundress eight years earlier are restated. The hospital wanted to take on the work of a home for foundlings "in order to save the life of the body and the soul, to provide a Christian education for them, and to prepare them to earn an honest living." They counted "on Providence and the charity of the faithful "to assure its success. On their return from foster homes, the children would remain at the hospital where the Sisters would be responsible for their upbringing until they reached eighteen years of age. If they then decided to continue in the employment of the hospital, they would draw a salary. Otherwise they would be free to "provide for themselves elsewhere" since they had been prepared to do other kinds of work.

By way of encouragement, Governor Gage decided to contribute the funds received from legal

---

10. Facts related by Faillon, p. 186.

fines, but this was a temporary measure, since the restoration of civilian government would put an end to it. It appears, however, that Marguerite's venture made a deep impression not only on the General but also on Mrs. Gage who apparently showed interest in it. When the official was promoted to the post of Governor of New York, Mme d'Youville wrote to him: "We are offering our poor prayers for the preservation of your health, the fulfilling of all your hopes, as well as for your wife and all your family, who are very dear to us and whom we shall always remember." [11] We can see in these letters a real expression of friendship and not simply a courteous formality. Other excerpts from her letters prove that for Marguerite courtesy was not the same as currying favor. Straightforward and sincere, she was "incapable of disguising the truth". She knew, however, how to recognize real worth and praise it. Helping her to do "some small good" would always evoke her gratitude.

The undertaking of a work of such scope during difficult times was certainly not inspired by human prudence. Only one earthly hope remained; like her contemporaries, she believed that the situation was temporary, and that when the warring parties had come to a settlement, France would keep its American colony. Therefore she specified in her report that the agreement "will last two years." At the end of this time, the colony would once again be under the authority of the French king. Then they would try

---

11. Letter of Dec. 29, 1763. Gage must have used great discretion in the term of office for, with the exception of "the bad storm" which threatened his relationship with the Sulpicians involving mixed marriages, his administration was marked by no dramatic event.

to make a permanent agreement. It was simply a matter of holding fast until the signing of the peace treaty. But this was a difficult task, and Marguerite found herself faced with serious financial difficulties, as were the two other communities of women in Montreal. [12] Obviously, it would have been easier for her to confine her attention to the sufferings which claimed her. But to do this, she would have had to ignore the basic requirements of her vocation; to see a brother in the man ready for the grave and that man of tomorrow still in the cradle and to help both of them.

For two years the provisional agreement remained in effect and only the abundant harvest of 1762 [13] — a real gift of Providence — encouraged them. The material conditions of the hospital were improved by this but it was still true that, in France, nothing had changed. And, faced with this silence, the Foundress became alarmed; one might almost say that she sensed what would happen to the colony. In 1762, began the series of letters she would hastily write to her friends and lawyers in France. These letters cover the last ten years of her life. Brief as they are, except for some addressed to friends, they still let us glimpse her thoughts, her chief worries.

"The holier a woman is, the more fully she is a woman," wrote Léon Bloy. As Marguerite walked farther along this mysterious way in which the Spirit guided her, the traits of her personality became more evident. In this valiant woman whom nothing daunted we can easily discern sensitivity, understanding and sympathy, for she remained the woman

---

12. Trudel, M., op. cit. 1, p. 326 and p. 341.
13. Ibid., p. 358.

she was even while giving herself completely to the profound work of grace. How easy it must have been to engage in conversation with her, for she did not drag out her remarks about her personal misfortunes, although she was not afraid to admit that she suffered. Certainly she was under no illusions concerning the dangers to the faith in this postwar period. She knew of the defections in the ranks of the clergy, of the scandalous love affairs which were the talk of the town, [14] and of the conflicts between the Church and the British over mixed marriages. Mme d'Youville did not discuss the details of these delicate situations, for this would have been contrary to her sense of discretion. But it is easy to see that they were her major concern. She wrote to the Superior of the Sulpicians that the return of M. Montgolfier "filled with joy those by whom he is loved and respected." [15] The undeniable influence of the vicar general and his cordial relationship with Governor Gage led her to hope for the future.

But the following year, when the news arrived that Canada had been ceded to England, [16] and the extent of the restrictions imposed by the Treaty of Paris became clear, [17] Marguerite returned to the

---

14. Among them, we might mention that of the McKay brothers with Mme and Mlle Herbin, who were descendants of Pierre Boucher and thus relatives of Marguerite. One of them, Francis McKay married M.-A. de Ligneris, grand-daughter of François d'Youville's half-sister and Marguerite's god-child, probably before a Protestant minister.

15. Letter to M. Louis Cousturier, Sept. 16, 1762.

16. The treaty was signed Feb. 10, 1763 and arrived in Canada the following May.

17. On the question of the problems of the Church at the time, one should read the excellent work of M. Trudel: *L'Église*

question. She admitted to M. Cousturier: "The situation in which we find ourselves makes us realize each day how much we are indebted to your goodness in the persons of these priests, the Sulpicians. Not merely our house but the whole colony is in a position to feel keenly how much we need the continuation of your kindnesses." [18]

Murray's opposition to the appointment of a bishop, the prohibition of admitting new members imposed on the Recollets and on the Jesuits, the mistrust of the British government for French priests are well known facts; and Mme d'Youville's fears were justified. Nevertheless, she continued to believe that the survival of the Church in Canada would depend largely on the Sulpicians.

Burdened with material worries, she did not think of restricting her works of charity. "If we are as free as we have been under English rule to practice our religion and to do all the good there is to be done, we will have no reason to complain of our spiritual situation; but as for our material circumstances there will be still more suffering. We do not have a way of earning our living under the English, as we could with the French; but I hope that Providence will supply our needs" she wrote to the Superior of the Society of the Foreign Missions, in Paris. [19]

Did she suspect that soon the future of the communities of women would be in jeopardy? We cannot

---

canadienne sous le régime militaire. Unless otherwise stated, the details relative to this matter have been taken from this work.

18. Letter of July 26, 1763.
19. Letter to M. Villars, Aug. 5, 1763.

say. At any rate, September 12, 1763, she asked Mr. Montgolfier, then in Quebec, for permission "to give the habit to three postulants who will be lay-sisters and to receive three others who have asked to be admitted." To support her request, she recalled to the vicar general that "Bishop de Pontbriand gave written permission to accept three girls who will have the rights of the administrators only at the death of the latter." [20] Humbly she added: "You know better than anyone else our needs; you know moreover that, of the twelve of us, almost half are no longer able to work."

But when she listed the works which would fall to new members, Marguerite showed most clearly how much the things of God concerned her. "The care of foundlings will require at least three Sisters; one for the new-born; one for toddlers; and a third for those whom we must teach." [21] The agreement with Governor Gage had run out; but nothing could stand in the way of her determination. M. Montgolfier, who had been elected bishop of Quebec but whose appointment was to remain secret, did not think it wise to grant this authorization. The Foundress answered him: "I will abide by what you tell me regarding our postulant-novices. They, as well as many others, will impatiently await your return. Your long and unwilling stay in Quebec leads us to fear lest the remainder of your trip be the same. For

---

20. Dec. 12, 1759, Bishop de Pontbriand himself authorized the religious profession of three Grey Nuns. At the time the Bishop was living in Montreal. In 1763, the number of Grey Nuns had increased to 15 and the last three to make profession were probably considered to be lay Sisters.

21. Quoted by Faillon, p. 261, who states in a notation that this is an original letter, addressed to M. Montgolfier.

myself, I will be consoled for it if you succeed."[22]
Another hope which would be shattered. Murray
was to oppose categorically the nomination of
M. Montgolfier, even when London would have
virtually accepted it. When the news had crossed
the Atlantic, another problem would be the order
of the day; the preservation of religious communities. In the autumn of 1763, d'Eon wrote to the Duc
de Choiseul: "We do not know what religious system
the English will set up in Canada; but there is no
doubt that, although they will permit the practice of
the Catholic religion, they will suppress the orders
of men and women at the same time, for they consider
them useless in the colony." [23]

During the crisis of 1752, Marguerite had written:
"If the Court of France approves our remaining
here..." And now, twelve years later, she experienced the same uncertainty. "Will they let us remain
here?" she wrote in substance to M. Montgolfier
on January 2, 1764. What will it be like tomorrow,
she seemed to wonder. "How will we get along, how
will we live under the English? They have done us
neither good nor evil until now. It is hard for us
to support ourselves... These people (the English)
do not provide work and their King even less." [24]
She had really only one certainty. "With God, nothing
is lost." [25] For the King of France was to devaluate
the war debts completely as a result of the lawsuit
brought against Bigot, the speculator, and his accom-

---

22. Letter of Oct. 4, 1763.
23. Ministry of Foreign Affairs, England, supplement of 1763.
24. Letter to M. Débarras, Sept. 16, 1764.
25. Letter to same, Sept. 16, 1764.

plices. [26] On the other hand, the Foundress' foresight regarding the Sulpicians' role in the survival
of the Church was justified on April 29, 1764. M.
Cousturier and his Council deeded the possessions
of the Society in Canada to the Sulpicians who agreed
to become British subjects. The mail brought the
news to Canada in June of the same year. [27] We
can guess at Marguerite's great joy, but this joy was
soon countered by the resignation of Mr. Montgolfier
on September 9, 1764, less than a year after his election. He stood aside in favor of M. Olivier Briand,
who was approved by Governor Murray. This
appointment would fill the vacancy in the episcopal
see. Everything remained in uncertainty, however,
and the disaster which struck Montreal on May 18,
1765 and which engulfed the hospital only worsened
the situation. Nevertheless, when she stated her
fears to the abbé de l'Isle-Dieu four months later,
she did not even allude to this fire. "Ask God, Father,
to give me the strength to bear all these crosses well
and to use them well. There are many of them, all
at once; losing one's king, one's country, one's
possessions and worst of all, to be afraid of seeing
one's holy religion die out." [28] There we have, in
her own words, her scale of values in comparison
with her faith. And since she saw everything in

---

26. Casgrain, H.-R.: *Les Sulpiciens et les Prêtres des Missions Étran-
    gères en Acadie* (1676-1762), 2, p. 422. The trial ended Dec. 10,
    1763. Bigot and Varin were exiled in perpetuity from France
    and the others were sentenced to make restitution of sums
    from thirty thousand to six hundred thousand pounds.

27. The document was received at the Registre de Quebec,
    Tuesday, June 11, 1765 at one o'clock and recorded Saturday,
    June 15 at 12:30.

28. Letter of Sept. 18, 1765. In this context, it is evident that
    Mme d'Youville referred to the devaluation of the war debts.

this light, we can understand her joy when, August 20, 1766, she confided to Mme de Ligneris: "Now we have a bishop. It seems probable that religion will be supported and maintained in this country. Many young men have asked to become priests since the arrival of his Excellency. [29] He has allowed a Sister of the General Hospital to pronounce her vows." [30] And further: "There is real hope that the religious communities will be supported. Things seem to go well for our religion...We must hope that God will pour out his blessings on this poor country. I recommend it to your prayers and to those of all your acquaintances." Thus she wrote to M. Charles Héry. His son, also named Charles, is said to have expressed a desire to become a priest before his departure for France. This urged Mme d'Youville to add: "I hope that in a few years you will send Charles back to help his country spiritually." [31] This request, which seems like a piece of advice, is surprising in Marguerite's writing for she was no preacher of morals. In her correspondence, we find very few words of advice; and those are addressed to her niece, Josette, who seemed to ask for them. But concerning the return to the country of Canadian priests she wrote openly to Mme de Ligneris: "You inform me that M. l'abbé Joncaire has decided to come here. He has not yet arrived and there is no word that he is

---

29. Bishop Briand was consecrated in Paris, March 16, 1766 and returned to Canada June 28, 1766.

30. This was Sr. B.-F. Prud'homme, Grey Nun, who pronounced her vows April 22, 1766.

31. Letter of Aug. 20, 1766. The young man must have changed his mind for, Sept. 24, 1770, Mme d'Youville wrote to the same correspondent "I am curious to find out about Charlot — whether he is studying, or whether he is going into business".

coming. I believe he made the decision in God's sight but that when it was a question of carrying it out his courage failed him." [32]

We might imagine her saying: The fate of the Church is assured, God has done his part. Now we must do ours.

---

32. Letter of Aug. 20, 1766. François d'Youville's half-sister had married a gentleman named de Joncaire. Probably the priest in question was his grandson and so related to the writer and to her correspondent. The priest did return to Canada but only for a short time, since he left in the Fall of 1766. (Letter of Mme d'Youville to the abbé de l'Isle-Dieu, Oct. 12, 1766).

Chapter XI

FATHER, THE HOUR HAS COME... (Jn. 17:1)

Marguerite's chosen way of perfection was to let herself be formed by the cross and to serve despite age, fatigue and obstacles. [1] The effort to go beyond the limits of one's selfishness, to give up everything [2] may involve many forms of renunciation, but it has one advantage. Because she never stopped concerning herself with the suffering of others, because she tirelessly tried to help them, Marguerite's faults and weaknesses died of starvation. "Love, and do what you will," said St. Augustine. So this woman who was indifferent to no kind of misfortune went on loving. We must attribute her silence about the difficulties she met in her personal life, at least partly, to her charitable activities. There was no time for her to draw up the list of her victories and defeats. She was not surprised at having to fight against innate weaknesses and did not despair because she had to begin the battle over and over again. Filled with confidence in God's mercy [3] because she herself had

---

1. It is well to note that Mme d'Youville, writing to M. Montgolfier, Oct. 4, 1763, digressed to say of one of her boarders: "She seems to care a great deal about reaching perfection". The fact did not escape her attention and gave her joy.
2. Original Commitment, art. 1.
3. Mother Despins, Marguerite's successor, in a letter to the abbé de l'Isle-Dieu, Sept. 10, 1772.

to ask for it, Marguerite learned the teachings of divine wisdom: "The virtuous man must be kindly... teach us, when we judge, to reflect on your kindness and when we are judged, to look for mercy " (Wis. 12:19-22). From her correspondence and her contemporaries' testimony, it is not easy to discover what were stumbling blocks for her. Still, we can find some clues. She had learned the habit of providing for her household. It must have been hard for her to be dependent on others for she had been proud. As a woman of decision, she found it difficult to put up with administrative delays. Sensitive to injustice, she felt keenly those directed against the General Hospital. She would need heroic virtue in these areas where she had already had ample opportunity to learn patience.

"We need crosses in order to reach heaven", she confided one day to her niece. [4] And we must admit that she had all she could wish "in this poor country where God gives them abundantly." [5] The one which was to be hers in 1765 would be the final test of her faith, her trust, and her total abandonment into the hands of Providence. It was another act of God in her heart.

A fire broke out in Montreal, May 18, 1765, at about two o'clock in the afternoon. [6] Since "she found it hard to believe that God would not preserve this house which is the refuge of the poor", the Foundress sent "all those who were able to help" into the city. They returned only when the fire

---

4. To Mme de Figuery, Aug. 20, 1766.

5. To M. Savarie, her attorney, Sept. 18, 1765.

6. The details of the fire are found in Mme d'Youville's letters of 1765. Those which deal with her words, acts and deeds are recorded in Sattin, pp. 43-45.

threatened the hospital. [7] It was already too late. "We were reduced to cinders in a very short time," she noted. [8] What she does not mention, what witnesses vouched for, was her open welcome to this unexpected trial. "The Lord had given us everything, the Lord has taken everything from us; Blessed be His name forever," she cried out like Job. And when the fire stopped, leaving only the walls standing, Marguerite knelt and prayed to "her usual source of help". "Father, whose majesty is infinite, we praise you." With her Sisters she said the Te Deum. She must have recited this prayer of praise often, for she recited it from memory. "In you, O Lord, I have placed my trust; let me not be confounded forever." Prayer restored peace to her soul. She got to her feet to house the poor and their servants in the buildings at Pointe-St-Charles. M. Montgolfier did not agree. He told her that he wanted her to go to the Hotel-Dieu where everything was ready to welcome these victims of the fire. [9] But Marguerite was aware of the destitution of the Nursing Sisters of St. Joseph who even considered returning to France after the fall of Canada. [10] It was not easy for her to impose this added burden on them, for an unspecified time. But she gave in, "like an obedient daughter and did not permit herself the least afterthought." [11]

---

7. To M. C. Héry, June 15, 1765.

8. To Mme de Ligneris, June 10, 1765.

9. Mme d'Youville mentioned 119 patients (letter to M. Héry, June 15, 1765) and 120 (letter to M. Goguet, the same day). However, the list she drew up June 27, 1765 shows 114 persons (Angers, pp. 332-333) so there must have been several deaths between May 18 and June 27.

10. Trudel, M., op. cit., 2, p. 330.

11. Sattin, p. 45.

The Foundress had just completed another stage in her spiritual journey. Until then, she had tried to see the evidence of the Lord's will in the cross. In this dramatic event, she accepted the fact that she did not understand, and spoke of the event as "God's good pleasure." [12] From laborious submission, Marguerite had come to total acceptance in spite of the mystery she could not penetrate. Here was the serenity of soul which belongs to those who know that they are in the hands of the best of Fathers. We might call this a foretaste of the happiness of those who mourn, while they know they will be consoled. To be convinced of this, she had only to study her own life. The trials of the past appeared in their true light. They had been God's work, preparing her soul for the influx of grace; the Father's revelation as He consoled her in her unhappy marriage; the persecution of the people of Montreal which made their support even more precious later; the fire of 1745 which urged her toward a total gift of self; Bigot's decree, ordering the suppression of her work which ended by the approbation of the community. The Lord delighted, it seemed, in piling up complicated situations which he then untangled later just at the time when everything seemed lost. How could she doubt that once again he would intervene in her favor since He had allowed adversity to touch her?

"The fruit of hope is abandonment to the Father"; abandonment for Marguerite was not passive submission but rather full and total cooperation. As she had done twenty years earlier, but in even more uncertain circumstances, she began to rebuild the

---

12. The expression "it pleased the Lord" which she used only once Sept. 16, 1764, recurs along with similar expressions rather frequently thereafter.

hospital. How touching it is to see this woman, then sixty-four years old, take up the task and display astonishing energy in it. To anyone who might have wished to express his admiration at this, she would probably have replied: "I am doing only what I should." [13]

But she accomplished this day by day, in uncertainty and insecurity. To collect the indemnity from the Court of France was the only guarantee she could count on to rebuild the hospital without contracting fresh debts. [14] Here, too, it pleased God to reduce her hopes to nothing. Gradually she would learn of the devaluation of "our paper money" and finally she realized that she could no longer hope for "any indemnity from the Court." [15] In France, Canadian creditors were considered to be speculators, and the Foundress did not hesitate to say: "We have been confused with those who have done a great wrong to the King of France. All the religious communities in this country are victims of this, and many honest persons have been ruined by it; the innocent are paying for the guilty." [16] Bigot, furthermore, had never agreed to reimburse the expenses in full, so that the hospital still owed a considerable deficit. [17] Marguerite was not deceived by this any more than by the other injustice relative to the sewing they had

---

13. To M. C. Héry, Sept. 24, 1770. After writing: "I do not know how my sister (Mme I. Gamelin) and her son hold up under the care they must provide for Ignace Gamelin, a chronic invalid, she added: "All the same, they are only doing what they ought".
14. Letter to M. Savarie, July 22, 1765.
15. Letter to the abbé de l'Isle-Dieu, July, 1769.
16. Letter to M. Maury, Sept. 21, 1770.
17. Letter to M. Savarie, Aug. 17, 1766. In this letter Mme d'Youville mentions taking out a loan to make up the deficit.

done for the French army. "The Intendant did not increase the price although he paid twice as much for them at the warehouse." [18] Faced with the irrevocable decree, the Foundress commented: "This is yet another fire for our poor and for ourselves." [19] "The Court is very hard-hearted; it is doing us a great wrong. May God forgive them." [20] And again this sentence which speaks volumes concerning her feelings for France: "In the end, the good King of France will keep everything. I would have no regrets if we returned to France, as people sometimes try to convince us." [21]

In these few words Marguerite revealed her vulnerability to suffering, but she did not let herself be overcome by it. "We have begun to rebuild, hoping that Providence, which has always sustained us, will continue to do so," she wrote to the abbé de l'Isle-Dieu, June 9, 1765, three weeks after the fire. Her hope, this time, would not be deceived. Unexpected and unhoped for help came from appeals for money made in London. The Foundress did not hesitate to say that "without this help the hospital would never have been rebuilt." She saw God's hand in this and cried out: "Providence is admirable; it has incomprehensible ways to relieve its members; it provides for everything; in it is all my trust." [22] This disclosure gives us a glimpse of the climate of her soul, absolutely certain that the Lord would not let her work be destroyed even if that should require

---

18. Letter to the abbé de l'Isle-Dieu, Oct. 17, 1768.
19. Letter to M. Savarie, Sept. 18, 1765.
20. Letter to the abbé de l'Isle-Dieu, July 1769.
21. Letter to Dr. A.-F. Feltz, Sept. 22, 1770.
22. Letter to the abbé de l'Isle-Dieu, Oct. 17, 1768.

miracles. So we need not be surprised at the strength she revealed, particularly in the letters written after the fire. She alluded to her misfortune only three times, and in very cursory fashion. "It has pleased God to try us by fire," she was careful to indicate. [23] To other correspondents she said: "I will not go into the details of this incident." [24]

If, by her own admission, she could not believe that the fire would destroy her house, [25] still she did not waste time in lamenting her misfortune. "What could we do about this? What we have tried to do as best we could, is to adore the designs of Providence and submit to his will," she confided to one of her benefactors. [26] Her niece, Josette, expressed her sympathy, and the Foundress comforted her: "I know your kind heart too well not to know how you suffer with us, but the matter is over. You must think no more of it," she advised. [27]

Marguerite did not want people to commiserate with her; but she herself had lost none of her ability to see herself in another's situation. This made her sensitive to others' sufferings. Her letters to Mme de Ligneris are evidence of this. The lady grieved that her daughter, Marie-Anne or Nanette had contracted a marriage with Francis McKay outside the Church. It seems that the mother asked Mme d'Youville to keep an eye on the young woman who was her godchild. Marguerite did not fail to do so. In 1764, the year of Mme de Ligneris' departure for France, she

23. Letter to M. Savarie, July 22, 1765.
24. Letter to M. Héry, June 15, 1765.
25. Letter to the abbé de l'Isle-Dieu, June 9, 1765.
26. Letter to M. St-Sauveur, Nov. 5, 1765.
27. Letter to Mme de Figuery, Aug. 1766.

wrote to her: "I would like to be able to tell you that Nanette is here, but we felt it advisable not to admit her here until she can no longer remain where she is." [28] This letter did not receive an answer. Marguerite returned to the matter, June 10, 1765, and expressed her sorrow at not having any news. Tactfully she announced that Nanette was pregnant and mentioned that, henceforth, the McKays would live outside the city because of the fire of May 18. This led the Foundress to speak of the fire. And we might be tempted to smile on reading the very feminine details she added: "You have lost your lovely dress. It was in a cupboard where there were many fine things." [29]

Some months later, the Foundress admitted to her correspondent: "You have no doubt, I think, of the pleasure I felt when I saw you here with our whole family; but the longer I live, the more delighted I am to know that you are in France and I should like to see my whole family there. The love I feel for them will never bring me to keep them here." [30] What an eloquent admission, from a woman who twice cried out at the departure of a member of her family and of a friend: "I do not have the courage to say goodbye to them." [31]

But then she had to announce Nanette's death to Mme de Ligneris. Marguerite showed greater tact, sensitivity and compassion than ever. She slipped her letter into one addressed to Dr. Feltz, asking him to

---

28. Letter of Oct. 1764.
29. Letter of June 10, 1765. Mme de Ligneris, Mme d'Youville's niece by marriage, stayed at the General Hospital before sailing for France.
30. Letter of Aug. 28, 1765.
31. Letters to E.-G. de Figuery, Sept. 16, 1762 and to M. Héry, Oct. 15, 1764.

prepare the recipient for the bad news. For her part, she went into great detail concerning the last moments of the young woman. "She suffered with heroic patience, received all the sacraments and she herself asked for the last anointing. Her husband and his brother did everything possible so that she would lack nothing, either spiritually or physically. They are in a state of sorrow that I cannot describe to you." [32] As for the McKay children: "They are in the care of their uncle; do not worry about them," urged the Foundress and continued: "Nanette, incapacitated since mid-April, always needed night-nurses, whom she found here at the hospital." Once again she added a feminine touch: "M. McKay has given her lovely dress to the church at LaPrairie." The irregularities of the mail delivery prevented this letter from reaching its destination, a fact which Mme d'Youville regretted the following September.

Sharing the sufferings of others led Marguerite to share her graces with them. To her nephew, Étienne-Guillaume de Figuery, who wrote to her to hasten Josette's departure for France, [33] the Foundress wrote that it was absolutely impossible for the Gamelins to assume the cost of the trip. She was surprised that the family was able to manage during the last three years without any source of income. There was no earthly source of hope. So the Foundress added: "We must hope, my dear nephew, that Providence, which always provides for the needs of those who are its servants, finds a way, either here or there, to provide for your dear wife what she needs to rejoin

---

32. Letter of Sept. 23, 1770. At the time, mixed marriages were not encouraged, but they were tolerated and held to be valid.

33. Josette Gamelin was Guillaume de Figuery's wife and Mme d'Youville's niece.

you." [34] To this young couple, settled in France, she wrote these revealing lines in 1766: "The perfect union that I see among you, dear Josette and your brother, delights me. Is there a joy in life greater than that of a happy home? All the goods of earth cannot approach it. I thank God for the grace He is giving you and I am begging him ardently to continue it and to increase it. You must not believe that there will not be crosses; we must have them in order to go to heaven. But united as all three of you are, you will be strong enough to bear them and to use them well." For Josette she included a personal message which concluded: "Farewell, my dear niece, I do not forget you nor those near you before God; and I beg Him that we may all be together in a blessed eternity."

As we read these excerpts, we might think this was the voice of a person who lived removed from the world, whose solitude was rarely disturbed. But this is a servant, the servant of the poor, whose life was devoted to work and who rejoiced to see her work intensified. "This year, we have begun to have a great deal of work," she wrote to M. Héry on June 15, 1765, "and I hope that Providence will give us the means of rebuilding." In fact, Providence did answer her prayer; and in December of the same year, they did move back to the hospital "where we are very badly off. We shall not lack ways of doing penance but we need them and we will strive to make good use of them." [35] Here, too, her expectations were fulfilled.

---

34. Letter of Aug. 5, 1763.
35. Letter to the abbé de l'Isle-Dieu, Aug. 28, 1765.

But one marvelous, inexpressible reality remained; the grace which took possession of her forty
years before [36] and which, since that time, had led her
along the path of trust, self-giving and love.

---

36. Letter to same, Oct. 12, 1766.

Chapter XII

THAT ALL MAY BE ONE... (Jn. 17:21)

"The hospital has been rebuilt as good as before," Marguerite wrote in 1770. But she added: "We shall not have as much linen for the poor and for ourselves at once," [1] for she always gave priority to the poor. The purchase of the estate at Chateauguay, three weeks after the fire, was also intended to improve the condition of her poor. [2] Despite the fire of 1765, "things seem to be going along well," the survival of the Church and religious communities was certain. Further, the Foundress emphasized: "We have begun to have a great deal of work". [3] This reassuring prospect almost totally evaporated, however, and as she lamented the fact, Marguerite mentioned: "Here, we do not have as much work as before. The poor are

---

1. Letter to M. Héry, Sept. 24, 1770.
2. At the request of Mlle M.-A. de Lanoue, co-owner of the estate, Mme d'Youville had cultivated the farm since 1751-1752. (Memorandum from Mother McMullen, S.G.M., p. 8). Despite the fire, she did not feel she could withdraw the promise to purchase the farm which she had made in 1764. To pay the debt, she used part of her patrimony and part of the patrimony of Sr. Despins. She was obliged, further, to sell the lands at Chambly which were less productive and the cause of many difficulties; the landowner and seven co-owners shared the property. (Letter of Mme d'Youville to Bishop Briand, Sept. 26, 1766).
3. Letter to M. Héry, June 15, 1765.

more and more numerous and everything is in short supply." [4] Some days earlier she had confided to the abbé de l'Isle-Dieu: "We have only one third as much work since the English have taken over." [5]

The financial appeals in London were certainly very helpful and the Foundress saw in them the action of Providence. However, they were not enough and despite her desire not to go into debt, the Superior was obliged to contract a debt of fifteen thousand pounds from the Seminary. "M. Montgolfier has done and continues to do more than I would have ever dared to ask of him," she wrote to the Superior General of the Sulpicians. [6] It pleased God to ask of her still another kind of renunciation. Until this time, she had provided for the needs of the poor by the work of her hands. Now she would have to decide to beg. From the appeals in London some seven thousand pounds remained in the agents' treasury. A request from Bishop Briand would be enough to urge the Governor General to contribute it to the hospital. Marguerite asked the Bishop to plead her case for her. She went ahead, and these lines prove that her love for the destitute won out over her pride. "There is much good to be done if we had the means," she wrote. "Every day poor people come who are truly in need. We have no more room and I send them away with a heavy heart but that is what I must do... If I knew where there was any money and I could get it without stealing it, I would quickly build a building to house almost two hundred. But I have nothing. The Lord will be satisfied with my good will." [7] Hearing

---

4. Letter to same, Sept. 24, 1770.
5. Letter of Sept. 20, 1770.
6. Letter to M. Cousturier, Aug. 21, 1766.
7. Letter to Bishop Briand, Sept. 22, 1769.

her, one would say that all she had left was the desire to do good. This desire knew no fatigue and explains why the Foundress was so insistent on collecting her debts from the war. It also explains her repeated requests to her lawyers and her friends in France. Courtesy, appreciation, gratitude and understanding are evident in these letters; so it is understandable that when she visited the patients in the hospital, they tried to keep her with them.

Delays and uncertainties in the mail did not make things any easier for her. Some letters were lost and two of her lawyers died within a short time of each other [8] and were replaced by M. J.-L. Maury in 1767. [9] Then once again she had to explain matters at length and resign herself to wait at least a year for the reply to know if they had been understood. When errors did occur, rectifying them was a complicated business. Mme d'Youville discovered one made by M. de Paris in the accounts for the year 1761-1762 which had escaped the vigilance of M. l'abbé de l'Isle-Dieu. She mentioned it to M. Savarie, adding: "It is possible that I am mistaken. Do not mention it to him, if he does not mention it to you, if you think it would distress him. He has rendered us too many services to contradict him in anything." [10] The vicar general, it seems, realized the error and mentioned it during 1764. The Foundress answered, "The deceased (M. de Paris) did his best to serve us

8. MM. de Paris and Savarie.

9. Mme d'Youville also wrote to the abbé de l'Isle-Dieu, Vicar General of the diocese of Quebec, to the Superior General of the Sulpicians, M. L. Cousturier; and to M. Villars, Superior of the Foreign Mission Society as well as to M. C. Héry, Dr. A.-F. Feltz, M. St-Sauveur, and M. Goguet, devoted friends who had returned to France.

10. Letter of Aug. 5, 1763.

and we should be very ungrateful if we tried to bother his family. No, assure them to the contrary and even if it applied only to you we consider him no longer in our debt before God and man, and we are praying for the repose of his soul." [11]

Two years later, the Foundress wrote to the same correspondent: "How can you concern yourself about an error of four or five hundred pounds, which may perhaps not even be an error, when you have rendered us services we cannot repay and which we will never forget nor will those who come after us." [12] It should be noted that she wrote these lines as she regretfully mentioned her lack of resources. Nor did she expect to leave the services of her lawyers unpaid. "These efforts should not go without payment," she explained in the case of M. Savarie. "I beg you, sir, to note this; I will approve everything you can do for him." [13] And she reminded M. Maury, "I do not see any entry for your fee. I ask you to include one." [14]

In her expressions of gratitude, the Foundress expressed her whole soul and unknowingly revealed the quality of her life of union with God. Christ had become her fulfillment, her other self, the Way in which she walked in complete trust. [15] Spontaneously she stated this to the vicar general of Quebec, her usual confidant, in a letter to which we must always return: "We are under obligations to you that

---

11. Letter of Sept. 16, 1764.
12. Letter of Aug. 22, 1766. This is probably not the error mentioned above.
13. Letter to M. Villars, Sept. 18, 1765.
14. Letter of Sept. 20, 1769.
15. This was the doctrine found in her bedside book: *La Dévotion au Sacré-Coeur de Jésus*, by Croiset, p. 104 — a devotion on which she meditated with profit.

we could never repay unless we could draw on the limitless treasury (of grace). As members of Jesus Christ, we have the means of repaying you for the good you have done for us. Often the Sisters and I beg our divine Savior and His Father who has been the object of my trust for almost forty years, to repay you." [16]

Quite simply, the Foundress let her heart overflow and we learn from her when, if not how, the event occurred which transformed her life. This very important disclosure explains it completely and is corroborated by the testimony of her contemporaries [17] who heard her recommend the devotion to the Eternal Father [18] to them and who especially admired the effects of this devotion in her. Because she believed in God's fatherhood, Marguerite saw a brother in each of the members of the human family especially in those who suffer or who are looked down on. And because she kept her eyes on Christ, the Beloved of the Father, she knew that love is proven by the spiritual and corporal works of mercy, the very basis for her religious family.

Even if her desires exceeded her fulfillment of them, Marguerite could not help but see the success of her work. The hospital was overflowing with the poor, [19] once it was almost completely rebuilt. The "church was not completed", but the two chapels added during the war and dedicated to the Eternal Father and to the Sacred Heart were once again

---

16. Letter of Oct. 12, 1766.
17. Dufrost, 2nd manuscript, p. 24.
18. Archives of the Grey Nuns, file of Sr. B.-F. Prud'homme.
19. She herself mentioned the presence of 170 persons in the hospital, in her letter of Sept. 22, 1770.

erected. [20] For the Grey Nuns they stood as a reminder of the Lord's words: "No one comes to the Father except through Me" (Jn. 14:6); "No one can come to Me unless the Father who sent Me draws him" (Jn. 6:44). To the Foundress, this recalled the prayer of her youth: "I come to You, Eternal Father, through the Heart of Jesus, my way, my truth, my life."

And a farmhouse, a mill, a bakery and a house for the employees were built on the land at Chateauguay and Pointe St-Charles. [21] The Superior herself supervised the construction and the Sisters came upon her, more than once, kneeling in prayer "in a nook", continuing her dialogue with God. [22] At Chateauguay she became the apostle of children and of ordinary people. She taught catechism to the children and explained to them the truths of faith, especially the one which nourished her own soul, the love of God the Father. Their attention could not be completely the effect of the snacks she gave them, once the lesson was over. Nor had she lost the ability to talk with the very young for she still provided shelter for orphans and foundlings. At the end of her busy days, the farmers, servants and lay people of the surrounding area met at her invitation. Together they spoke of God, ending the evening with prayer. [23] Marguerite adapted her teaching to them, close as they were to the soil. So she wrote: "From May 10 to July 18 we have had almost continuous rain; we thought everything would be lost. But, thanks to Divine Providence, there is a rather fine crop of

---

20. Faillon, p. 223; the church was dedicated Aug. 30, 1767.
21. Financial records of the hospital.
22. Faillon, pp. 286-287.
23. Fauteux, Sr. A., *La Vénérable Mère d'Youville*, p. 164.

wheat." [24] Her listeners realized that God the Father provides for man's needs.

But Marguerite conveyed especially to her companions the truth which lit up her life; she knew she was freely loved by God. She was sure of the "Lord who is so good and so merciful to us". [25] The word 'us' alone indicates her sense of community. And she invited her Sisters to "cast all their cares into the bosom of God."

She showed a special affection with esteem, respect, trust and gratitude to the Sisters who had borne the heat of the day with her as well as to those who had joined their group later. Their common effort had made the creation and support of the community possible. More than anyone else, the Foundress knew what courage they had needed to endure the early days of persecution. Gentleness and the persuasiveness of her example (for she never required of others what she had not first done herself) sealed the unity of the small group of Sisters.

But gentleness in Marguerite did not soften into weakness. When Sister Céloron, a novice, injured herself fatally by lifting a load too great for her strength, the Superior did not allow her to pronounce her vows publicly. It is believed, however, that she did make private vows. [26] Marguerite believed that a Sister did not belong to herself and that she should take care of her health in order to serve the poor. Kindly with respect to failings which are beyond the power of human weakness, she was very strict with

24. Letter to Dr. Feltz, Aug. 25, 1768.
25. Letter to the abbé de l'Isle-Dieu, Sept. 22, 1770.
26. The entry into the Grey Nuns of the novice's mother, after her daughter's death, seems to support the tradition.

respect to faults against charity and mutual acceptance. She was convinced that the strength of a community is found precisely in unity among its members, and she insisted that love and forgiveness should have the last word. M. H. F. Gravé, superior of the Seminary of Quebec, saw her gifts as a religious superior when he wrote to Mother Despins: "It is not pleasant to be the immediate successor of a teacher and a superior who was loved so tenderly and whose worth was so unusual. (It is like) being the successor to another Jane Frances de Chantal. I have no hesitation in comparing them. In fact, on reading the latter's biography, in many places one need only change the names to recall Mme d'Youville's life." [27]

And yet, like other founders and foundresses of religious communities, Marguerite did have some failures. The seed she sowed did not always fall into good ground. And this was to be the trial of her final days. Still, because she found the strength to love in spite of everything, she was able to correct without flinching or to be silent when faced with what could not be changed. "A person closely related to her by birth", [28] her son, François d'Youville, the priest, was a cause of bitter suffering to her. As pastor of St-Ours parish, he built the parish church from 1753 to 1755 and, for that purpose, borrowed nine thousand pounds from Mme d'Youville. But then, he persisted in his refusal to repay the money despite his mother's financial difficulties, insisting that the money was rightfully his by inheritance. The disagreement was submitted to arbitration before three

27. Letter of Jan. 5, 1772. M. Gravé had taken on the post of hospital chaplain from 1759 to 1761.
28. Was this person Mme de la Gemeraye or her son François d'Youville? In our opinion, it can refer to either one.

persons chosen by the priest in 1763. But it was not resolved for he did not accept their decision. [29] The Foundress had used "the money of the poor" and so for her, it was a conflict of two loves. Her integrity toward the poor won out, and Marguerite appealed to Bishop Briand. The Bishop sent to Marguerite the summons to be relayed to the obstinate priest. She delayed sending it because, she explained, "My son has broken his left arm four inches from the shoulder; he has enough trouble for the moment." She hurried to his bedside, cared for him for three days and "sent him a Sister and one of the women boarders to carry on her services." The last sentence of this letter lets us glimpse how keenly François' stubbornness hurt her: "There are still so many things to say which would be too long to write." [30]

Yet another suffering was added to this one which few of her companions were aware. On this matter her writings tell us absolutely nothing. "Some of her Sisters pretended to show her great affection and tried to spread evil about her behind her back," Charles wrote. [31] Nothing escaped the Foundress' keen awareness but she maintained heroic silence, like the Master who had been betrayed Himself. She had

---

29. Mme d'Youville to M. Montgolfier, Aug. 5, 1763.

30. Letter of 1769, undated. It should be said, in François' defence, he paid the debt, but only after his mother's death. In 1770, Bishop Briand instructed M. Montgolfier to tell the Pastor of St. Ours that "His behavior toward his mother displeased him." (Archives of the Chancery of the Archdiocese of Montreal, file: correspondence of M. Montgolfier, Oct. 17, 1770).

31. 2nd manuscript, p. 27. This probably refers to Srs. Varambourville and Boisclair who would both leave the community, the first in 1771 to return the same year and leave again in 1775 and the second who left Oct. 16, 1791.

meditated on the cross, had taught how necessary it was, and now, as the time when God would call her to Himself drew nearer, she was to live out her teaching. And she was supported by companions whose loyalty was beyond doubt and who showed her the tenderest love. Her letters reveal the peace of soul enjoyed by those who look at things only in the light of eternity. Everything — crosses and joys — was the Lord's gift in her eyes. To Governor General Carleton who sent her foodstuffs for the poor she wrote; "I wonder at Providence which inspired you to do us this act of charity, seeing the needs of our hospital." Ever concerned about other people she added; "I would never have dared to ask you for anything, knowing that you have to give so much to various poor people whose need is great." [32]

Seeing the good works carried on at the hospital, she attributed them to God: "We are eighteen Sisters, all frail, who manage a house where there are one hundred seventy people to be fed and almost all of them to be provided for. Every day I wonder at Divine Providence which is willing to use such poor persons to do some small good." [33] And she did not exclude those of her Sisters who were a source of suffering for her from the good accomplished. Wishing to remind them of the duties of their way of life, she decided to have a retreat for the whole community in the Fall of 1770. [34] It would be preached by M. Montgolfier and would include the renewal of the Original Commitment, the promises in which she had synthesized the spirit of her Congregation. During this period of recollection, the Sisters medi-

---

32. Letter of June 18, 1770.
33. Letter to the abbé de l'Isle-Dieu, Sept. 22, 1770.
34. Montgolfier, Constitutions, p. 69.

tated before the painting of the Father, [35] on the litany composed by M. de Lavalinière at the Foundress' request and recited daily since April 4, 1770. [36] This litany praises "the Father of Wisdom and of Truth, Source of all consolation, of infinite love, who gave to the world His Son, who reveals to little ones the mystery of the cross and who sees those who adore him in spirit and in truth."

So each of the Sisters, even those who had already done so, signed the document and promised "for the greater glory of God and the salvation of (their) souls" to serve the poor. The retreat ended on October 23rd, the thirty-ninth anniversary of the day on which Marguerite became a member of the Confraternity of the Sacred Heart and set out on the road of love. How persuasive her advice to the Sisters must have been for they "never tired of hearing her." Now that they had had the opportunity to be renewed in the spirit which was to guide them, the Foundress left the future to the Lord. "God be praised, Divine Providence sees to everything; in it is all my trust," she probably repeated and would write some months later. [37]

Her own earthly future would not be long, she sensed. In fact, during the winter of 1771, she nearly died. In a letter written March 8, M. Montgolfier informed Bishop Briand that in view of her critical condition, he had decided to let Sister Martel of the Hôtel-Dieu take care of her as well as her usual doctor. On April 17 there was a further medical

---

35. The painting was saved from the fire of 1765 by M. de Féligonde with the help of one of the Sisters. The statuette of the Virgin was found in the ruins.

36. Faillon, pp. 279-280.

37. Letter to the abbé de l'Isle-Dieu, Sept. 21, 1771.

bulletin, more reassuring this time, since it seemed that her recovery was possible. But this recovery was jeopardized by the activities of Sister Varambourville who abandoned both the religious habit and the hospital. [38] Finally, on May 6, the Vicar General announced that "Mme d'Youville seems entirely recovered; all she needs is to further regain her strength." And to pardon, for Sister Varambourville returned to the fold, at the request of Charles Dufrost; the Foundress accepted her as a lay Sister. [39]

Strong and peaceful, Marguerite resumed her usual occupations, looking after the needs of the household. Her last letter addressed to Sir Guy Carleton, is the swan song of a soul concerned for the good of others. After congratulating him on his appointment to a second term, she said to him with an admirable freedom of spirit: "I hope that the good-will you have shown to the Canadians will accompany you on your return; I ask it of you, Sir, for our house and especially for the foundlings whom we have housed since we have been under British rule. I beg the honor of your patronage before His Majesty to obtain some help for these unfortunate little ones. I fear that we may have to give up this good work for lack of money to sustain it. You can foresee how much cruelty that would breed in those who would bury their shame with their children. This idea is strong enough to impress a compassionate and charitable heart. I hope that you will not refuse this favor." [40]

---

38. M. Montgolfier believed that Sr. Varambourville was mentally ill. (Letter to Bishop Briand, April 17, 1771).
39. Letter from M. Montgolfier to Bishop Briand, June 15, 1771.
40. Letter of Sept. 23, 1771, exactly three months before her death. 332 illegitimate children preceded her in death.

Marguerite's soul was still vigorous but her body was worn out. In November, she was forced to remain in her room and on December 9, she was stricken with a first attack of paralysis followed by a second attack four days later. Neither she nor those near to her could cherish any further illusions. By December 14, she had drawn up her will, dividing her patrimony between the poor and her sons. [41] She stipulated that the Superior of the Seminary would make decisions relative to her funeral and burial and begged for the prayers of her poor and her Sisters. The poor were still first in her thoughts, as was only right, for her life had been spent in serving them.

She advised her Sisters, whose attachment to her she knew well: "This is God's will, Sisters. I must submit to it, and so should you. God Himself is asking this sacrifice of you." [42] Later, she confided to them: "How happy I would be if I saw myself in heaven with all my Sisters."

Sister Coutlée, her nurse, slept in her room. M. de Féligonde, the hospital chaplain, suggested to her to put her cot in an adjoining room. She was deeply distressed, and the Foundress came to her rescue: "Oh, she will not do that; she will not have the courage to do it." Yet another indication of that concern for others which stayed with her until the end. Now, she asked that the small statue of Our Lady of Providence be brought to her; how often she had begged Our Lady to "pray for her now and at the hour of death." And Our Lady, who had witnessed that first consecration in 1737, would hear the last prayer

---

41. Mme d'Youville received only the income from her mother's estate, and her legacy went to her two sons who, then, left it to the other Lajemmerais heirs.

42. Faillon, p. 306.

of a woman who had tried, as she had, to conform her life to Christ's.

Speech had become increasingly difficult for her because of the paralysis, so she took advantage of a slight improvement to leave her Sisters a spiritual will:

"Dear Sisters, always be faithful to the duties of the way of life you have chosen. Always walk in the way of obedience to the rule of life, of obedience to authority, and of mortification. But above all, behave in such a way that the most perfect union will reign among you." [43]

Like the Master who also prayed for union among his disciples, Marguerite understood its importance and left it to her Sisters as the best way of following her.

Marguerite commended her soul into the hands of the Eternal Father on December 23, 1771, at about half past eight in the evening, at the age of seventy. She was "filled with trust in his mercy and conformity to His will." [44]

Three days later, the day after Christmas, her body was placed in the grave by the poor, assisted by the lay help; she was buried in the center of the crypt in a spot where her poor could see her grave from the gallery of the chapel.

"Our days dwindle...our lives are over in a breath; our life lasts for seventy years;...over in a trice, and then we are gone..."(Ps. 90:9-10). Everything had come to an end for the mother of the poor.

---

43. Sattin, p. 50. The details of Mme d'Youville's last days are found in this biography, pp. 49-51.

44. Mère Despins in a letter to the abbé de l'Isle-Dieu, Sept. 10, 1772.

Would her memory fade, like that of other mortals?

The Lord who exalts the humble would glorify his servant. On May 3, 1959, one hundred and eighty-eight years after her death, "the increasing fame of her holiness having been confirmed by miracles," His Holiness John XXIII would proclaim: "We have the joy of placing in the catalogue of the Blessed the name of this first flower of holiness to bloom on Canadian soil."

The spiritual portrait of Marguerite, would be sketched by Pope John as follows: "Marguerite d'Youville gave herself entirely to God Who infused into her soul especially the spirit of adoption which makes us cry out: 'Abba, Father!' All her thoughts, all her desires she then turned toward this all-loving heavenly Father and toward His poor and unfortunate earthly children." [45]

Thirty-one years later, on December 9, 1990, in St. Peter's Basilica in Rome, His Holiness John Paul II issued the solemn proclamation:

For the honor of the Holy Trinity, for the exaltation of the Catholic Faith, for an increase in Christian living, by the authority of Jesus Christ, the apostles Peter and Paul and our own, after having deliberated, implored God's help, asked the advice of many brethren, we decree and define that Blessed Marguerite d'Youville is a saint. We include her in the catalogue of Saints, thus establishing that she be among the Saints in the Church, the subject of our devotion.

In his homily, the Holy Father described the journey of Marguerite towards God, our Father through Jesus Christ, His Son, who, alone is the Way.

---

45. Pope John XXIII, Apostolic Letter, pp. 1-3.

"Marguerite d'Youville appears to us as a woman who heard the Lord say to her, "Give comfort to My people", "Make ready My way by going in search of the poorest, those whose lives have been one long, endless trail of suffering" (...) "Kindness and truth shall meet, justice and peace shall kiss" (Ps 84:11). Saint Marguerite d'Youville, in the Advent of the Church with all the saints you give us an image of the world in which Kindness, Truth, Justice and Peace reign. (...)

In her daily devotion Marguerite brought a little of that newness to the neediest: a community of love where the lowly are respected because the Lord is near to them, because He is present within their hearts. For the saint whom we are honouring, it is the daily concrete acts of charity which make God's justice triumph, and which reveal the presence of the new world. (...) More than once the work which Marguerite undertook was hindered by nature or by people. In order to work to bring that new world of justice and love closer, she had to fight some hard and difficult battles. The foundress of the "Grey Nuns" gives us a great example: she knew to overcome disappointments, to accept the suffering which she bore as a Cross together with Christ. Abandoning herself into the hands of Providence, Marguerite followed her path in hope. She never stopped trusting". (...) Marguerite placed her life completely in the hands of God the Creator, day after day, in a spirit of deep trust, she sought "to offer herself with Jesus to our Heavenly Father". (...) In God Marguerite saw the Father who "loved the world so much that He gave His only Son" (Jn 3:16).

In union with Our Lady of Providence, as she called the Mother of the Saviour, she would prayerfully contemplate the mystery of God's universal fatherhood: she came to understand that all men and women are truly brothers and sisters, that their heavenly Father would never fail to be close to them, and that His love called them to an active life of service to others. We thank God for the figure which He sets before our eyes this morning. Yes, we give Him thanks. For the first time in history, a woman of Canadian birth is inscribed among the Saints whom the Church has raised to the glory of the altars.''

This homage from the Church's highest authority implies the pre-eminent approval of a woman ''who having greatly loved Jesus Christ and served Him in the person of the poor'' is worthy of universal admiration.

May Saint Marguerite d'Youville obtain for the faithful, the grace to lend an ear to the message of Jesus: whoever welcomes one of these little ones in my name, welcomes Me and whoever welcomes Me, welcomes not only Me, but also the One who sent Me'' (Mk 9:37).

APPENDIX

Rule of the Grey Nuns
in effect since Jan. 1738

At five o'clock, the Sisters will rise at the first sound of the bell, make the sign of the cross on themselves and on their heart to impress there the love of Jesus' cross; they will adore God and thank Him for having preserved them during the night, asking his forgiveness for any faults they may have committed. They will offer themselves with Jesus to His Father in order to spend the day in His love, and they will say the names of Jesus and Mary.

They will recall the subject of meditation in order to prepare themselves to meditate well; they will kneel down for a moment to adore the Sacred Heart of Jesus and to venerate the name of Mary. They will kiss the floor to recall what they are now and what they will become.

At six o'clock, they will go in silence to hear Mass and to receive Communion on the days appointed. After Mass, they will go to serve the poor. As they enter the wards, they will, in the spirit of faith, recognize Christ in the person of the poor and they will show every possible deference. Joyfully they will serve their needs, patiently putting up with their moods, and, deaf to all repugnance, they will willingly go to serve those for whom they feel the greatest distaste.

At seven-thirty, they will begin work, after saying the Veni Sancte Spiritus and reading two verses of the Imitation of Christ. They will observe silence and will be sure to lift their hearts to God to offer them to Him in the spirit of penance.

At nine o'clock, they will have spiritual reading together for a quarter of an hour, after which they will keep sacred silence in order to be attentive only to God and the ways of growing in holiness.

At eleven-fifteen, they will have particular examen in common, which will begin with the reading of five or six verses of Scripture, followed by the Veni Sancte Spiritus, after which they will examine themselves on the virtue they should practice or the fault they should avoid. They will conclude by reciting the Sub Tuum.

After dinner, they will go to church in silence to say the Angelus and to adore Our Lord.

Recreation will last until one o'clock. They will be careful not to give way to too great levity and never to speak uncharitably. Rather, remembering the presence of God, they will discuss only things which may serve to edify or to refresh the mind.

At five o'clock, they will serve the poor and then recite in common the Office of the Name and Coronation of the Blessed Virgin, followed by the rosary.

They will retire at nine-thirty, after making the sign of the cross, kissing the floor, offering their rest to God and uniting themselves to the hearts of Jesus and Mary, and recommending themselves to the care of their guardian angel.

They will have great respect for each other, along with sincerity. They will never address one another with too much familiarity. They will avoid any relationships which might be detrimental to charity.

Attitudes with which
the Sisters should act

They should keep secret all the customs and practices of the house, even with the most intimate and prudent persons.

They should give no external sign nor speak in any way which would lead others to think they wish to form a new community. However, they will strive to live by faithfully practicing the following virtues: a perfect union, all forming one heart and one soul, each foreseeing the needs of others and bearing with love the faults of others, realizing that others need even greater love to bear her failings.

All-embracing poverty, keeping nothing individually but holding everything in common, gratefully accepting what others have the generosity to give us, like Jesus, who, though he was absolute Lord of all, had nowhere to lay his head.

A deep humility, always considering oneself to be less than the others, having a poor opinion of oneself, wondering at how others can put up with someone so filled with faults.

Submission and blind obedience to Superiors, doing nothing without permission and keeping every part of the Rule.

A childlike simplicity in speech and in conduct, concerned only with one's own duties, not prying into what others are doing, not rationalizing about what one is asked to do and not refusing what is requested.

Wholehearted sincerity, making known one's

illnesses, and one's needs, not hiding one's weaknesses.

Continual mortification, especially by curbing one's willfulness, overcoming one's moods, one's desires, and one's levity, and by taking advantage of opportunities to mortify oneself. But all this should be done without too much tension nor forced effort.

Boundless love for the poor, always attentive to their needs, not being annoyed at their moodiness, seeing in them Jesus Christ whose members they have the honor to be.

Although they may not form a new community, they will conduct themselves in the house, externally and even more by the interior dispositions of the heart as though they were living a consecrated life. Hence, those who wish to consecrate themselves to the service of the poor and to join those who are there now can be received as postulants. They will be expected to observe the rule exactly for a certain length of time, in order to determine whether they are apt subjects for the house and if they believe themselves capable of fulfilling its duties.

They will be faithful to avoid doing anything which might injure their health.

Complete text of the original commitment

We, the undersigned, for the greater glory of God, the salvation of our souls and the relief of the poor, sincerely desiring to leave the world, renouncing everything we own to consecrate ourselves unreservedly to the service of the poor, have joined together in the bonds of the purest charity, not wishing of ourselves to form a new community, in order to live and die together. In order that this union may be solid and permanent, we have unanimously agreed and have freely promised of our own will what follows:

To live henceforth together for the remainder of our lives in perfect union and charity, under the guidance of those (superiors) who will be given to us, in the practice and faithful observance of the rule prescribed for us; in submission and complete obedience to the one among us who will be entrusted with the government of the house; in poverty and complete renunciation, henceforth placing everything we now own and will own in common, not retaining ownership nor any right to dispose of it, making a pure, simple and irrevocable gift of it to the poor by this document, for neither any of us nor our relatives can have any claim on it after our death for whatever reason, excepting, however, our patrimony, if there is any, of which we can dispose as we wish.

To devote unreservedly our time, our days, our effort, our life itself to work, and, putting the income in common, to provide for the support and maintenance of the poor.

To shelter, feed and support as many poor people as we can either by our own means or by the alms of the faithful.

All those who will be taken into the house will bring everything they own with them — linens, clothing, furniture and silver, to put everything in common not excepting or retaining anything, renouncing all rights of ownership and of retention, by the voluntary and irrevocable gift they will make of it to the members of Jesus Christ; but if they have income or annuities, they also will be included and placed in the common fund. Only their patrimony is excepted, as stated above, which they may dispose of at their death.

If one of those accepted into the house is obliged to leave for a good reason, she cannot demand anything that she brought with her, since she voluntarily renounced it and gave it to the poor when she entered. She will be satisfied with what we will have the generosity to give her.

If, in the future, there should no longer be persons capable of continuing this good work, or if, for some other good reason, it is thought that it should not continue, the undersigned wish and intend that all possessions, furnishings and buildings belonging to this house be handed over to the Superior of the Seminary of Montreal, to be used as he thinks best for works of charity and particularly for the relief of the poor; all rights of ownership should be handed over to him and given over as stated above: both in their own name and in the name of the poor to whom everything belongs; once again they declare that this is their intention.

Having read and re-read the act of union, we approve it and commit ourselves to carry out all it contains with our whole heart and with the grace of the Lord.

Given at Montreal, in the presence of the undersigned, Feb. 2, 1745.

N.B. *The documents: Rule, Attitudes and Original Commitment were initialed and approved by Bishop de Pontbriand, June 15, 1755.*

BIBLIOGRAPHY

ANGERS, Mme Albertine Ferland
Mère d'Youville, 1701-1771
Fondatrice des Soeurs de la Charité de l'Hôpital
général de Montréal, dites Soeurs Grises, Montréal
Librairie Beauchemin, Limitée, 1945.

BABIN, P., o.m.i.
Dieu et l'adolescent
Collection «Chemins de la Foi»
Éditions du Chalet, Lyon, 1964.

BÉGON, Mme E. Michel
Correspondance
Rapport de l'Archiviste de la Province de Québec,
1934-1935
Redempti Paradis
Imprimeur de Sa Majesté le Roi, 1935.

BONNEFONS, Rv. Amable, S.J.
Le petit livre de vie qui apprend à bien vivre et
à bien prier Dieu
A Paris, Chez J.-B. Delespine, imp. lib.,
à la Victoire et au Palmier
MDCCXLIX, approbation et privilège du Roy.

BOUDON, Henri-Marie, docteur en théologie et
grand archidiacre de l'église d'Évreux
Les Saintes Voies de la Croix
A Paris chez J.-B. de Lespine, imprimeur et libraire
ordinaire du Roi, rue St-Jacques, à l'image de
St Paul 1716, avec approbation et privilège.

BOURDALOUE, Père, S.J.
Retraite spirituelle à l'usage des communautés religieuses
A Paris, G. Martin, à l'étoile d'or
MDCCL avec approbation et privilège du Roy.

CASGRAIN, l'Abbé, H.-R.
Guerre du Canada, 1756-1760.
Montcalm et Lévis
2 tomes
Québec, Imprimerie de L.-J. Demers et Frère
30, rue de la Fabrique, 1891.

CASGRAIN, l'Abbé H.-R.
Les Sulpiciens et les prêtres des Missions-étrangères en Acadie (1676-1762)
Québec, Librairie Montmorency-Laval
Pruneau & Kirouac, libraires-éditeurs
46, rue de la Fabrique, 1897.

CHAMPAGNE, Antoine
Les La Vérendrye et le Poste de l'Ouest
Les Cahiers de l'Institut d'histoire
Les Presses de l'Université Laval
Québec, 1968.

COLLABORATION (En)
Dictionnaire biographique canadien
Volume II
De 1701 à 1740
Les Presses de l'Université Laval, 1969.

CROISET, P. Jean, S.J.
La dévotion au Sacré Coeur de Jésus
Imprimé à Paris, Josse, 1737.

DROUIN (Institut généalogique)
Dictionnaire national des Canadiens-français
1608-1760
4184, rue St-Denis, Montréal, Can. 1965.

FAILLON, Étienne-Michel, p.s.s.
Vie de Mme d'Youville, fondatrice des Soeurs de
la Charité de Ville-Marie, dans l'Île de Montréal,
en Canada.
Ville-Marie, chez les Soeurs de la Charité
Hôpital général, 1852.

FAUTEUX, Sr Albina, s.g.m.
L'Hôpital général des Soeurs de la Charité
(Soeurs Grises) depuis sa fondation jusqu'à
nos jours
Tome premier 1692-1821
Imprimerie des Soeurs Grises
Montréal 1916.

FITTS, Sister Mary, G.N.S.H.
Hands to the Needy
Garden City, New York
Doubleday & Company Inc., 1950.

FRÉGAULT, Guy, de l'Académie canadienne-
française
Le XVIIIe siècle canadien
Études
Collection Constantes, volume 16
Éditions HMH, Montréal, 1968.

GOSSELIN, Abbé Auguste
L'Église du Canada après la conquête
1er volume:
Québec, Imprimerie Laflamme
34, rue Garneau 1916
2e volume publié en 1917.

JAMET, Dom Albert, o.s.b.
Marguerite Bourgeoys, 1620-1700, 2 volumes
1942, Île de Montréal
La Presse catholique Panaméricaine.

MITCHELL, Estelle, s.g.m.
Elle a beaucoup aimé
Vie de la Bienheureuse Marguerite d'Youville,
fondatrice des Soeurs de la Charité, «Soeurs grises»
1701-1771, 17e mille
Fides
Montréal et Paris, 1959 et 1960.

MITCHELL, Estelle, s.g.m.
Mère Jane Slocombe, neuvième supérieure générale
des Soeurs Grises de Montréal, 1819-1872
«Fiat, le plus beau mot».
Fides, Montréal et Paris, 1964.

MITCHELL, Estelle, s.g.m.
Messire Pierre Boucher, écuyer, seigneur de
Boucherville, 1622-1717
Montréal, Librairie Beauchemin Limitée, 1967.

RICHAUDEAU, l'Abbé
Lettres de la Rév. Mère Marie de l'Incarnation,
première supérieure du monastère des Ursulines
de Québec, 2 tomes
Vve H. Casterman
Éditeur pontifical, imprimeur de l'Évêché Tournai,
1876.

RUTLEDGE (Joseph Lister)
Century of Conflict
Garden City, New York
Doubleday and Co. Inc., 1956.

TRUDEL, Marcel, D. ès L.
L'Église canadienne sous le Régime militaire
1759-1764
I — Les problèmes
Les Études de l'Institut d'Histoire de l'Amérique
française, 1956.

TRUDEL, Marcel, D. ès L.
L'Église canadienne sous le Régime militaire
1759-1764.
II — Les Institutions
Les presses universitaires Laval, Québec 1957.

TRUDEL, Marcel, D. ès L.
L'Esclavage au Canada français
Histoire et conditions de l'esclavage
Les Presses universitaires Laval
Québec, Canada, 1960.

VERHEYLEZOON, Louis, S.J.
La dévotion au Sacré-Coeur
Éditions Salvator, Mulhouse, 1954.

TABLE OF CONTENTS

Imprimé par IMPRIMERIE QUEBECOR LEBONFON

Printed in Canada